A Choice of
KIPLING'S VERSE
made by T. S. Eliot

This volume is published by special arrangement
with Messrs. Methuen & Co., Ltd., and
Messrs. Macmillan & Co., Ltd.

A Choice of
KIPLING'S VERSE

made by
T. S. ELIOT

with an essay on
RUDYARD KIPLING

faber and faber

First published in December 1941
by Faber and Faber Limited
3 Queen Square, London W.C.1.
First published in this edition 1963
Reprinted 1970, 1973, 1976, 1979 and 1983
Printed in Great Britain by
Richard Clay (The Chaucer Press) Ltd,
Bungay, Suffolk

ISBN 0 571 05444 7

RUDYARD KIPLING

There are several reasons for our not knowing Kipling's poems so well as we think we do. When a man is primarily known as a writer of prose fiction we are inclined—and usually, I think, justly—to regard his verse as a by-product. I am, I confess, always doubtful whether any man can so divide himself as to be able to make the most of two such very different forms of expression as poetry and imaginative prose. I am willing to pay due respect, for instance, to the poetry of George Meredith, of Thomas Hardy, of D. H. Lawrence as part of their *œuvre*, without conceding that it is as good as it might have been had they chosen to dedicate their whole lives to that form of art. If I make an exception in the case of Kipling, it is not because I think he succeeded in making the division successfully, but because I think that, for reasons which it will be partly the purpose of this essay to put forward, his verse and his prose are inseparable; that we must finally judge him, not separately as a poet and as a writer of prose fiction, but as the inventor of a mixed form. So a knowledge of his prose is essential to the understanding of his verse, and a knowledge of his verse is essential to the understanding of his prose. In so far therefore as I concern myself here with his verse by itself, it is only with the aim of restoring it to its place

5

afterwards and seeing the total work more clearly. In most studies of Kipling that I have read, the writers seem to me to have treated the verse as secondary, and in so doing to have evaded the question—which is, nevertheless, a question that everyone asks—whether Kipling's verse really is poetry; and, if not, what it is.

The starting point for Kipling's verse is the motive of the ballad-maker; and the modern ballad is a type of verse for the appreciation of which we are not provided with the proper critical tools. We are therefore inclined to dismiss the poems, by reference to poetic criteria which do not apply. It must therefore be our task to understand the type to which they belong, before attempting to value them: we must consider what Kipling was trying to do and what he was not trying to do. The task is the opposite of that with which we are ordinarily faced when attempting to defend contemporary verse. We expect to have to defend a poet against the charge of obscurity: we have to defend Kipling against the charge of excessive lucidity. We expect a poet to be reproached for lack of respect for the intelligence of the common man, or even for deliberately flouting the intelligence of the common man: we have to defend Kipling against the charge of being a 'journalist' appealing only to the commonest collective emotions. We expect a poet to be ridiculed because his verse does not appear to scan: we must defend Kipling against the charge of writing jingles. In short, people are exasperated by poetry which they do not understand, and contemptuous of poetry which they understand without effort; just as an audience is offended by a speaker who talks over its head, and by a speaker whom it suspects of talking down to it.

A further obstacle to the appreciation of many of Kipling's poems is their topicality, their occasional character, and their political associations. People are often inclined to disparage poetry which appears to have no bearing on the situation of to-day; but they are always inclined to ignore that which appears to bear only on the situation of yesterday. A political association may help to give poetry immediate attention: it is in spite of this association that the poetry will be read, if it is read, to-morrow. Poetry is condemned as 'political' when we disagree with the politics; and the majority of readers do not want either imperialism or socialism in verse. But the question is not what is ephemeral, but what is permanent: a poet who appears to be wholly out of touch with his age may still have something very important to say to it; and a poet who has treated problems of his time will not necessarily go out of date. Arnold's *Stanzas from the Grande Chartreuse* voice a moment of historic doubt, recorded by its most representative mind, a moment which has passed, which most of us have gone beyond in one direction or another: but it represents that moment for ever.

We have therefore to try to find the permanent in Kipling's verse: but this is not simply to dissociate form from content. We must consider the content itself, the social and political attitude in its development; and, making an effort to detach ourselves from the assumptions of our own generation, enquire whether there is something more in Kipling than is expressed by Beerbohm's caricature of the Bank Holiday cornet virtuoso on the spree.

I

In the selection which follows I have found no place for the earliest of Kipling's published verse: to be precise, the selection begins from page 81 of the Collected Edition. The earlier work is juvenilia, but juvenilia which, having been published in its time and had a success in its time, is essential reading for a full understanding of Kipling's progress. Most of it is what it was intended to be, light reading in an English newspaper in India: it exhibits that same

7

precocious knowingness about the more superficial level of human weakness that is both effective and irritating in some of his early stories of India. It is obviously the work of a clever young man who might go far in journalism, but neither in feeling nor in rhythm does most of it give any hint that the author would ever write a memorable poem. It is unnecessary to say that it is not poetry: what is surprising and interesting is that it does not pretend to be poetry, that it is not the work of a youth whom anyone would suspect of any aspiration to write poetry. That he is gifted, that he is worth watching, is obvious when you know how young he is: but the gift appears to be only for the ephemeral, and the writer appears to aim at nothing higher.

There were, however, literary influences in the background. We have among his verse a pastiche of *Atalanta in Calydon* made for his own immediate purposes; we remember also that McIntosh Jellaludin (who is introduced as falling over a camel foal while reciting *The Song of the Bower*) on one occasion recited the whole of *Atalanta* beating time with a bedstead leg. There was Kipling's family connection with Pre-Raphaelite society: and Kipling's debt to Swinburne is considerable. It is never an imitation: the vocabulary is different, the content is different, the rhythms are different. There is one early monologue which is much more closely imitated from Browning than anything is imitated from Swinburne: but it is in two poems extremely unlike Browning's in style—*McAndrew's Hymn* and *The 'Mary Gloster'*—that Browning's influence is most visible. Why is the influence of Swinburne and Browning so different from what you would expect? It is due, I think, to a difference of motive: what they wrote they intended to be poetry; Kipling was not trying to write poetry at all.

There have been many writers of verse who have not aimed at writing poetry: with the exception of a few

8

writers of humorous verse, they are mostly quickly forgotten. The difference is that they never did write poetry. Kipling does write poetry, but that is not what he is setting out to do. It is this peculiarity of intention that I have in mind in calling Kipling a 'ballad-writer' and it will take some time to make clear what I mean by that. For I am extending and also somewhat limiting the meaning of the word 'ballad'. It is true that there is an unbroken thread of meaning connecting the various kinds of verse to which the term 'ballad' has been applied. In the narrative Border Ballad, the intention is to tell a story in what, at that stage of literature, is the natural form for a story which is intended to arouse emotion. The poetry of it is incidental and to some extent unconscious; the form is short rhymed stanzas. The attention of the reader is concentrated on the story and the characters; and the ballad must have a meaning immediately apprehensible by its auditors. Repeated hearings may confirm the first impressions, may repeat the effect, but full understanding should be conveyed at one hearing. The metrical form must be of a simple kind which will not call attention to itself, but repetitions and refrains may contribute an incantatory effect. There should be no metrical complications corresponding to subtleties of feeling that cannot be immediately responded to. At another stage of culture—as in Anglo-Saxon and in the elaborate forms of Welsh—poetry develops a conscious virtuosity, requiring a virtuosity of appreciation on the part of the audience: the forms impose upon the bard restrictions and obstacles in overcoming which he exhibits his skill. It must be remembered that this sophistication is not only present in what we call 'modern' literature or in the later stages of development of classical literatures such as those of Latin, Greek, Sanskrit, Persian, or Chinese: it is a stage sometimes reached in the poetry of peoples of lower cultures. And on the other hand, ballad verse is not simply a stage in historical development: the ballad persists and develops in its own way, and corresponds to a permanent level of enjoyment of literature. There is always a potential public for the ballad: but the social conditions of modern society make it difficult for the good ballad to be written. It is perhaps more difficult now than it was at the time when *Barrack Room Ballads* were written: for Kipling had at least the inspiration and refreshment of the living music-hall.

In order to produce the contemporary ballad, it is of no particular help to hold advanced social views, or to believe that the literature of the future must be a 'popular' literature. The ballad must be written for its own sake and for its own purposes. It would be a mistake, also, and a supercilious kind of mistake, to suppose that the audience for balladry consists of factory workers, mill hands, miners and agricultural labourers. It does contain people from these categories, but the composition of this audience has, I suspect, no relation to any social and economic stratification of society. The audience for the more highly developed, even for the more esoteric kinds of poetry is recruited from every level: often the uneducated find them easier to accept than do the half-educated. On the other hand, the audience for the ballad includes many who are, according to the rules, highly educated; it includes many of the powerful, the learned, the highly specialised, the inheritors of prosperity. I do not mean to suggest that the two audiences ought to be, or must be, two worlds: but that there will be one audience capable only of what I may call ballad attention, and a smaller audience capable of enjoying both the ballad and the more difficult forms of poetry. Now it is to the ballad attention that Kipling addresses himself: but that does not mean that all of his poems appeal only on that level.

What is unusual about Kipling's ballads is his singleness of intention in attempting to convey no more to the simple minded than can be taken in on one reading or hearing.

10

They are best when read aloud, and the ear requires no training to follow them easily. With this simplicity of purpose goes a consummate gift of word, phrase, and rhythm. There is no poet who is less open to the charge of repeating himself. In the ballad, the stanza must not be too long and the rhyme scheme must not be too complicated;[1] the stanza must be immediately apprehensible as a whole; a refrain can help to insist upon the identity within which a limited range of variation is possible. The variety of form which Kipling manages to devise for his ballads is remarkable: each is distinct, and perfectly fitted to the content and the mood which the poem has to convey. Nor is the versification too regular: there is the monotonous beat only when the monotonous is what is required; and the irregularities of scansion have a wide scope. One of the most interesting exercises in the combination of heavy beat and variation of pace is found in *Danny Deever*, a poem which is technically (as well as in content) remarkable. The regular recurrence of the same end-words, which gain immensely by imperfect rhyme (*parade* and *said*) gives the feeling of marching feet and the movement of men in disciplined formation—in a unity of movement which enhances the horror of the occasion and the sickness which seizes the men as individuals; and the slightly quickened pace of the final lines marks the change in movement and in music. There is no single word or phrase which calls too much attention to itself, or which is not there for the sake of the total effect; so that when the climax comes—

'What's that that whimpers over'ead?' said Files-on-
    Parade,
'It's Danny's soul that's passin' now,' the Colour-Sergeant
    said.

[1] Though Kipling could manage even so difficult a form as the sestina: see p. 45.

11

(the word *whimper* being exactly right) the atmosphere has been prepared for a complete suspension of disbelief.

It would be misleading to imply that all of Kipling's poems, or at least all that matter, are 'ballads': there is a great variety of kinds. I mean only that the approach to the understanding of what he was trying to do, in all his varied verse, is through the ballad motive. The best introduction, for my present purpose, is to call attention to a dozen or so particular poems representing his different types. For the reader to whom the ballad approach to poetry is the most natural, there is no need to show that Kipling's verse reaches from time to time the intensity of 'poetry': for such readers it is more useful to discuss the content, the view of life, and to overcome the prejudices which they may entertain against any verse which has a different subject matter or a different point of view from that which they happen to accept: to detach it, furthermore, from irrelevant association with subsequent events and attitudes. That I shall attempt in the next section. In choosing the examples which follow here, I have in mind rather the reader who, if he believes that Kipling wrote 'political jingles', stresses the word *jingles* rather than the word *political*.

The first impression we may take from inspection of a number of the poems chosen to show the variety, is that this variety is suspiciously great. We may, that is, fail to see in it more than the virtuosity of a writer who could turn his hand to any form and matter at will: we may fail to discern any unity. We may be brought to admit that one poem after another does, in one way or another, have its 'poetic' moment, and yet believe that the moments are only accidental or illusory. It would be a mistake to assume that a few poems can be chosen which are 'poetry', and that the rest, by implication, need not be read. A selection made in this way would be arbitrary, because there is no handful of poems which can be so isolated from the rest;

12

it would be misleading because the significance of the 'poems' would be lost except with the background of the 'verse', just as the significance of the verse is missed except in the context of the prose. No part of Kipling's work, and no period of his work, is wholly appreciable without taking into account the others: and in the end, this work, which studied piecemeal appears to have no unity beyond the haphazard of external circumstances, comes to show a unity of a very complicated kind.

If, therefore, I call particular attention to *Danny Deever* as a barrack-room ballad which somehow attains the intensity of poetry, it is not with the purpose of isolating it from the other ballads of the same type, but with the reminder that with Kipling you cannot draw a line beyond which some of the verse becomes 'poetry'; and that the poetry, when it comes, owes the gravity of its impact to being something over and above the bargain, something more than the writer undertook to give you; and that the matter is never simply a pretext, an occasion for poetry. There are other poems in which the element of poetry is more difficult to put one's finger on, than in *Danny Deever*. Two poems which belong together are *McAndrew's Hymn* and *The 'Mary Gloster'*. They are dramatic monologues, obviously, as I have said, owing something to Browning's invention, though metrically and intrinsically ballads. The popular verdict has chosen the first as the more memorable: I think that the popular verdict is right, but just what it is that raises *McAndrew's Hymn* above *The 'Mary Gloster'* is not easy to say. The rapacious old ship owner of the latter is not easily dismissed, and the presence of the silent son gives a dramatic quality absent from McAndrew's soliloquy. One poem is no less successful than the other. If the McAndrew poem is the more memorable, it is not because Kipling is more inspired by the contemplation of the success of failure than by that of the failure of success, but because there is greater poetry in the

13

subject matter. It is McAndrew who creates the poetry of Steam, and Kipling who creates the poetry of McAndrew.

We sometimes speak as if the writer who is most consciously and painstakingly the 'craftsman' were the most remote from the interests of the ordinary reader, and as if the popular writer were the artless writer. But no writer has ever cared more for the craft of words than Kipling: a passion which gives him a prodigious respect for the artist of any art, and the craftsman of any craft[1] and which is perhaps involved in his respect for Free Masonry. The problems of the literary artist constantly recur in his stories:[2] in *Wireless*, for instance, where the poor consumptive chemist's assistant is for a night identified with Keats at the moment of writing *The Eve of St. Agnes*; in *The Finest Story in the World*, where Kipling takes the trouble to provide a very good poem, in rather free verse (the *Song of the Galley Slaves* in this volume) and a very bad poem in regular verse, to illustrate the difference between the poem which forces its way into the consciousness of the poet and the poem which the writer himself forces. The difference between the craft and the art of poetry is of course as difficult to determine as the difference between poetry and balladry. It will not help us to decide the place of Kipling in poetry: we can only say that Kipling's craftsmanship is more reliable than that of some greater poets, and that there is hardly any poem, even in the collected works, in which he fails to do what he has set out to do. The great poet's craft may sometimes fail him: but at his greatest moments he is doing what Kipling

[1] *The Bull That Thought* in the bull-ring 'raged enormously; he feigned defeat; he despaired in statuesque abandon, and thence flashed into fresh paroxysms of wrath—but always with the detachment of the true artist who knows that he is but the vessel of an emotion whence others, not he, must drink'.

[2] In *Proofs of Holy Writ* (a story published in the *Sussex* edition only), Shakespeare and Jonson discuss a problem of choice of words put before them by one of the translators of the King James Bible. See also the poem on Shakespeare in this volume.

14

is usually doing on a lower plane—writing transparently, so that our attention is directed to the object and not to the medium. Such a result is not simply attained by absence of decoration—for even the absence of decoration may err in calling attention to itself—but by never using decoration for its own sake,[1] though, again, the apparently superfluous may be what is really important. Now one of the problems which arise concerning Kipling is related to that skill of craftsmanship which seems to enable him to pass from form to form, though always in an identifiable idiom, and from subject to subject, so that we are aware of no inner compulsion to write about this rather than that—a versatility which may make us suspect him of being no more than a performer. We look, in a poet as well as in a novelist, for what Henry James called the Figure in the Carpet. With the greatest of modern poets this Figure is perfectly manifest (for we can be sure of the existence of the Figure without perfectly understanding it): I mention Yeats at this point because of the contrast between his development, which is very apparent in the way he writes, and Kipling's development, which is only apparent in what he writes about. We expect to feel, with a great writer, that he *had* to write about the subject he took, and in that way. With no writer of equal eminence to Kipling is this inner compulsion, this unity in variety more difficult to discern.

I pass from the earlier ballads to mention a second category of Kipling's verse: those poems which arise out of, or comment upon topical events. Some of these, such as *The Truce of the Bear*, in the form of an apologue, do not aim very high. But to be able to write good verse to occasion is a very rare gift indeed: Kipling had the gift, and he took the obligation to employ it very seriously. Of this type of poem I should put *Gehazi*—a poem inspired

[1] The great speech of Enobarbus in *Antony and Cleopatra* is highly decorated, but the decoration has a purpose beyond its own beauty.

15

by the Marconi scandals—very high, as a passionate invective rising to real eloquence (and a poem which illustrates, incidentally, the important influence of Biblical imagery and the Authorised Version language upon his writing). The poems on Canada and Australia, and the exequy on King Edward VII, are excellent in their kind, though not very memorable individually. And the gift for occasional verse is allied to the gift for two other kinds of verse in which Kipling excelled: the epigram and the hymn. Good epigrams in English are very few; and the great hymn writer is very rare. Both are extremely objective types of verse: they can and should be charged with intense feeling, but it must be a feeling that can be completely shared. They are possible to a writer so impersonal as Kipling: and I should like the reader to look attentively at the *Epitaphs of the War*. I call Kipling a great hymn writer on the strength of *Recessional*. It is a poem almost too well known to need to have the reader's attention called to it, except to point out that it is one of the poems in which something breaks through from a deeper level than that of the mind of the conscious observer of political and social affairs—something which has the true prophetic inspiration. Kipling might have been one of the most notable of hymn writers. The same gift of prophecy appears, on the political plane, in other poems, such as *The Storm Cone*, but nowhere with greater authority than in *Recessional*.

It is impossible, however, to fit all of Kipling's poems into one or another of several distinct classes. There is the poem *Gethsemane*, which I do not think I understand, and which is the more mysterious because of the author's having chosen to place it so early in his collected edition, since it bears the sub-heading '1914–1918'. And there are the poems of the later period.

The verse of the later period shows an even greater diversity than the early poems. The word 'experimentation' may be applied, and honourably applied, to the work of many poets who develop and change in maturity. As a man grows older, he may turn to new subject-matter, or he may treat the same material in a different way; as we age we both live in a different world, and become different men in the same world. The changes may be expressed by a change of rhythm, of imagery, of form: the true experimenter is not impelled by restless curiosity, or by desire for novelty, or the wish to surprise and astonish, but by the compulsion to find, in every new poem as in his earliest, the right form for feelings over the development of which he has, as a poet, no control. But just as, with Kipling, the term 'development' does not seem quite right, so neither does the term 'experimentation'. There is great variety, and there are some very remarkable innovations indeed, as in *The Way Through The Woods* and in *The Harp Song of the Dane Women*—

> What is a woman that you forsake her,
> And the hearth-fire and the home-acre,
> To go with the old grey Widow-maker?

and in the very fine *Runes on Weland's Sword*. But there were equally original inventions earlier (*Danny Deever*); and there are too, among the later poems, some very fine ones cast in more conventional form, such as *Cold Iron*, *The Land*, *The Children's Song*.

I confess therefore that the critical tools which we are accustomed to use in analysing and criticising poetry do not seem to work; I confess furthermore that introspection into my own processes affords no assistance—part of the fascination of this subject is in the exploration of a mind so different from one's own. I am accustomed to the search for form: but Kipling never seems to be searching for form, but only for a particular form for each poem. So we find in the poems an extraordinary variety, but no evident pattern—the connection is to be established on

17

some other level. Yet this is no display of empty virtuosity, and we can be sure that there is no ambition of either popular or esoteric success for its own sake. The writer is not only serious, he has a vocation. He is completely ambidexterous, that is to say completely able to express himself in verse or prose: but his necessity for often expressing the same thing in a story and in a poem is a much deeper necessity than that merely to exhibit skill. I know of no writer of such great gifts for whom poetry seems to have been more purely an instrument. Most of us are interested in the form for its own sake— not apart from the content, but because we aim at making something which shall first of all *be,* something which in consequence will have the capability of exciting, within a limited range, a considerable variety of responses from different readers. For Kipling the poem is something which is intended to *act*—and for the most part his poems are intended to elicit the same response from all readers, and only the response which they can make in common. For other poets—at least, for some other poets—the poem may begin to shape itself in fragments of musical rhythm, and its structure will first appear in terms of something analogous to musical form; and such poets find it expedient to occupy their conscious mind with the craftsman's problems, leaving the deeper meaning to emerge, if there, from a lower level. It is a question then of what one chooses to be conscious of, and of how much of the meaning, in a poem, is conveyed direct to the intelligence and how much is conveyed indirectly by the musical impression upon the sensibility—always remembering that the use of the word 'musical' and of musical analogies, in discussing poetry, has its dangers if we do not constantly check its limitations: for the music of verse is inseparable from the meanings and associations of words. If I say then, that this musical concern is secondary and infrequent with Kipling, I am not implying any inferiority of craftsmanship, but rather a different order of values from that which we expect to determine the structure of poetry.

If we belong to the kind of critic who is accustomed to consider poems solely by the standards of the 'work of art' we may tend to dismiss Kipling's verse by standards which are not meant to apply. If, on the other hand, we are the biographical critic, interested primarily in the work as a revelation of the man, Kipling is the most elusive of subjects: no writer has been more reticent about himself, or given fewer openings for curiosity, for personal adoration or dislike.

The purely hypothetical reader who came upon this essay with no previous acquaintance with Kipling's verse, might perhaps imagine that I had been briefed in the cause of some hopelessly second-rate writer, and that I was trying, as an exhibition of my ingenuity as an advocate, to secure some small remission of the penalty of oblivion. One might expect that a poet who appeared to communicate so little of his private ecstasies and despairs would be dull; one might expect that a poet who had given so much of his time to the service of the political imagination would be ephemeral; one might expect that a poet so constantly occupied with the appearances of things would be shallow. We know that he is not dull, because we have all, at one time or another, by one poem or another, been thrilled; we know that he is not ephemeral, because we remember so much of what we have read. As for shallowness, that is a charge which can only be brought by those who have continued to read him only with a boyish interest. At times Kipling is not merely possessed of penetration, but almost 'possessed' of a kind of second sight. It is a trifling curiosity in itself that he was reproved for having placed in defence of the Wall a Roman Legion which historians declared had never been near it, and that later discoveries proved to have indeed been stationed

19

there: that is the sort of thing one comes to expect of Kipling. There are deeper and darker caverns which he penetrated, whether through experience or through imagination does not matter: there are hints in *The End of the Passage*, and later in *The Woman in His Life* and *In the Same Boat*: oddly enough, these stories are foreshadowed by an early poem which I have not included, *La Nuit Blanche*, which introduces one image which reappears in *The End of the Passage*. Kipling knew something of the things which are underneath, and of the things which are beyond the frontier.[1]

I have not explained Kipling's verse or the permanent hold that it can have upon you. It will be enough if I can help to keep him out of the wrong pigeon-holes.[2] If the reader of this book denies that Kipling is a great writer of verse, I hope at least that he will have found new reasons for his judgement, for the ordinary charges brought against him are either untrue or irrelevant. I have been using the term 'verse' with his own authority, for that is what he called it himself. There is poetry in it; but when he writes verse that is not poetry it is not because he has tried to

[1] Compare the description of the agony in *In the Same Boat* (a story the end of which is truer to the experience than is the end of *The Brushwood Boy*): 'Suppose you were a violin string—vibrating—and someone put his finger on you' with the image of the 'banjo string drawn tight' for the breaking wave in *The Finest Story in the World*. Compare also the story *A Matter of Fact* (of the submarine volcanic eruption which projects the sea-monster to the surface) with the opening passages of *Alice in Wonderland*: both depict external events which have exact nightmare correspondence to some spiritual terror. *A Matter of Fact* is a better story than *In the Same Boat*, for the psychological explanation in the latter story comes as an anti-climax to the experience.

[2] Dr. J. H. Oldham has drawn my attention to the relevance of the chapter on 'Art and Magic' in that very remarkable book, *The Principles of Art*, by Professor R. G. Collingwood. Collingwood takes Kipling as an example of 'the artist as magician', and defines a magical art as 'an art which is representative and therefore evocative of emotion, and evokes of set purpose some emotions rather than others in order to discharge them into the affairs of practical life'. Professor Collingwood's contribution here seems to me extremely valuable; but while Kipling is a very good example of what he calls 'the artist as magician', I do not feel that 'the artist as magician' is a complete description of Kipling as a writer of verse.

20

write poetry and failed. He had another purpose, and one to which he adhered with integrity. It is expressed in a poem (from *A Diversity of Creatures*) which I have thought would come with more effect at the end of this section of my essay, than in the body of the book:

THE FABULISTS
1914–1918

When all the world would keep a matter hid,
　　Since Truth is seldom friend to any crowd,
Men write in fable as old Æsop did,
　　Jesting at that which none will name aloud.
And this they needs must do, or it will fall
Unless they please they are not heard at all.

When desperate Folly daily laboureth
　　To work confusion upon all we have,
When diligent Sloth demandeth Freedom's death,
　　And banded Fear commandeth Honour's grave—
Even in that certain hour before the fall,
Unless men please they are not heard at all.

Needs must all please, yet some not all for need,
　　Needs must all toil, yet some not all for gain,
But that men taking pleasure may take heed,
　　Whom present toil shall snatch from later pain.
Thus some have toiled, but their reward was small
Since, though they pleased, they were not heard at all.

This was the lock that lay upon our lips,
　　This was the yoke that we have undergone,
Denying us all pleasant fellowships
　　As in our time and generation.
Our pleasures unpursued age past recall,
And for our pains—we are not heard at all.

21

What man hears aught except the groaning guns?
　　What man heeds aught save what each instant brings
When each man's life all imaged life outruns,
　　What man shall pleasure in imaginings?
So it has fallen, as it was bound to fall,
We are not, nor we were not, heard at all.

II

I have expressed the view that the variety of Kipling's
verse and its mutations from one period to another, can-
not be accounted for, and given a unified pattern, by
tracing development as we might with most poets. His
development cannot be understood through his verse
alone, because he was, as I said at the beginning, an integral
prose-and-verse writer; and to understand changes we
have to consider the prose and the verse together. Kipling
appears first to be a writer of different phases and occupa-
tions, who in each phase is completely developed, who is
never so committed to the pursuit of one verse form as to
be prevented from moving to another. He is so different
from other poets that the lazy critic is tempted merely to
assert that he is not a poet at all, and leave it at that. The
changes in his poetry, while they cannot be explained by
any usual scheme of poetic development, can to some ex-
tent be explained by changes in his outward circumstances.
I say 'to some extent', because Kipling, apparently merely
the reflection of the world about him, is the most inscrut-
able of authors. An immense gift for using words, an
amazing curiosity and power of observation with his mind
and with all his senses, the mask of the entertainer, and
beyond that a queer gift of second sight, of transmitting
messages from elsewhere, a gift so disconcerting when we are
made aware of it that thenceforth we are never sure when it
is *not* present: all this makes Kipling a writer impossible
wholly to understand and quite impossible to belittle.

22

Certainly an exceptional sensitiveness to environment is the first characteristic of Kipling that we notice; so that on one level, we may trace his course by external circumstances. What life would have made of such a man, had his birth, growth, maturity and age all taken place in one set of surroundings, is beyond speculation : as life directed, the result was to give him a peculiar detachment and remoteness from all environment, a universal foreignness which is the reverse side of his strong feeling for India, for the Empire, for England and for Sussex, a remoteness as of an alarmingly intelligent visitor from another planet. He remains somehow alien and aloof from all with which he identifies himself. The reader who can get a little distance—but not deep enough—below the level of Kipling's popularity as a teller of tales and reciter of ballads, and who has a vague feeling of something underneath, is apt to give the wrong explanation of his own discomfort. I have tried to disturb the belief that Kipling is a mere writer of jingles : we must now consider whether these 'jingles' are, in a denigratory sense, 'political'.

To have been born in India and to have spent the first remembered years there, is a circumstance of capital importance for a child of such impressionability. To have spent the years from seventeen to twenty-four earning his living there, is for a very precocious and observant young man an important experience also. The result is, it seems to me, that there are two strata in Kipling's appreciation of India, the stratum of the child and that of the young man. It was the latter who observed the British in India and wrote the rather cocky and acid tales of Delhi and Simla, but it was the former who loved the country and its people. In his Indian tales it is on the whole the Indian characters who have the greater reality, because they are treated with the understanding of love. One is not very loving between seventeen and twenty-four. But it is Purun Bhagat, it is the four great Indian characters in *Kim* who

23

are real: the Lama, Mahbub Ali, Hurree Chunder Moo-kerjee, and the wealthy widow from the North. As for the Britons, those with whom he is most sympathetic are those who have suffered or fallen—McIntosh Jellaludin has learned more than Strickland.[1] Kipling is of India in a different way from any other Englishman who has written, and in a different way from that of any particular Indian, who has a race, a creed, a local habitation and, if a Hindu, a caste. He might almost be called the first citizen of India. And his relation to India determines that about him which is the most important thing about a man, his religious attitude. It is an attitude of comprehensive tolerance.[2] He is not an unbeliever—on the contrary, he can accept all faiths: that of the Moslem, that of the Hindu, that of the Buddhist, Parsee or Jain, even (through the historical imagination) that of Mithra: if his understanding of Christianity is less affectionate, that is due to his Anglo-Saxon background—and no doubt he saw enough in India of clergy such as Mr. Bennett in *Kim*.

To explain Kipling's feeling for the Empire, and his later feeling for Sussex, as merely the nostalgia of a man without a country, as the need for support felt by the man who does not belong, would be a mistake which would prevent us from understanding Kipling's peculiar contri-bution. To explain away his patriotic feeling in this way is only necessary for those who consider that such feeling is not a proper theme for verse. There are perhaps those who will admit to expression in poetry patriotism on the defensive: Shakespeare's Henry V is acceptable, in his otherwise embarrassing grandiloquence, because the French army was a good deal bigger than the English

[1] On the subject of Kipling's ethics, and the types of man which he holds up for respect, see a valuable essay by Mr. Bonamy Dobrée in *The Lamp and the Lute*. My only criticism of this essay is that it does not take full account of Kipling's later work.

[2] Not the tolerance of ignorance or indifference. See *The Mark of the Beast*, which those who do not believe in the existence of the Beast prob-ably consider a beastly story.

force, even though Henry's war could hardly be described as a defensive one. But if there is a prejudice against patriotic verse, there is a still stronger prejudice against imperial patriotism in verse. For too many people, an Empire has become something to apologise for, on the ground that it happened by accident, and with the addition that it is a temporary affair anyway and will eventually be absorbed into some universal world association: and patriotism itself is expected to be inarticulate. But we must accustom ourselves to recognising that for Kipling the Empire was not merely an idea, a good idea or a bad one; it was something the reality of which he felt. And in his expression of his feeling he was certainly not aiming at flattery of national, racial or imperial vanity, or attempting to propagate a political programme: he was aiming to communicate the awareness of something in existence of which he felt that most people were very imperfectly aware. It was an awareness of grandeur, certainly, but it was much more an awareness of responsibility.

There is the question of whether 'political' poetry is admissible; there is the question of the way in which Kipling's political poetry is political; there is the question of what his politics were; and finally, there remains the question of what we are to say of that considerable part of his work which cannot, by any stretch of the term, be called political at all.

It is pertinent to call attention to one other great English writer who put politics into verse—Dryden. The question whether Kipling was a poet is not unrelated to the question whether Dryden was a poet. The author of *Absalom and Achitophel* was satirising a lost cause in retrospect, and he was on the successful side; the author of *The Hind and the Panther* was arguing a case in ecclesiastical politics; and both of these purposes were very different from that which Kipling set himself. Both of Dryden's poems are

more political in their appeal to the reason than any of
Kipling's. But the two men had much in common. Both
were masters of phrase, both employed rather simple
rhythms with adroit variations; and by both the medium
was employed to convey a simple forceful statement,
rather than a musical pattern of emotional overtones. And
(if it is possible to use these terms without confusion) they
were both classical rather than romantic poets. They arrive
at poetry through eloquence; for both, wisdom has the
primacy over inspiration; and both are more concerned
with the world about them than with their own joys and
sorrows, and concerned with their own feelings in their like-
ness to those of other men rather than in their particu-
larity. But I should not wish to press this likeness too far,
or ignore the great differences: and if Kipling suffers in
some respects by the comparison, it must be remembered
that he has other qualities which do not enter into it at all.

Kipling certainly thought of verse as well as prose as a
medium for a public purpose; if we are to pass judgement
upon his purpose, we must try to set ourselves in the his-
torical situations in which his various work was written;
and whether our prejudice be favourable or antagonistic,
we must not look at his observations of one historical
situation from the point of view of a later period. Also, we
must consider his work as a whole, and the earlier years
in the light of the later, and not exaggerate the importance
of particular pieces or phrases which we may not like.
Even these may be misinterpreted. Mr. Edward Shanks,
who has written the best book on Kipling that I have read
(and whose chapter on 'The Prophet of Empire' resumes
Kipling's political views admirably) says of the poem
called *Loot* (a soldier ballad describing the ways of extort-
ing hidden treasure from natives): 'this is wholly detest-
able, and it makes the commentator on Kipling turn red
when he endeavours to explain it'. This is to read an atti-
tude into the poem which I had never suspected. I do not

26

believe that in this poem he was commending the rapacity and greed of such irregularities, or condoning rapine. If we think this, we must also presume that *The Ladies* was written to glorify miscellaneous miscegenation on the part of professional soldiers quartered in foreign lands. Kipling, at the period to which these poems belong, undoubtedly felt that the professional ranker and his officers too were unappreciated by their peaceful countrymen at home, and that in the treatment of the soldier and the discharged soldier there was often less than social justice: but his concern was to make the soldier known, not to idealise him. He was exasperated by sentimentalism as well as by depreciation or neglect—and either attitude is liable to evoke the other.

I have said that in Kipling as a poet there is no development, but mutation; and that for the development we must look to changes in the environment and in the man himself. The first period is that of India; the second that of travel and of residence in America; the third is that of his settlement in Sussex. These divisions are obvious: what is not so obvious is the development of his view of empire, a view which expands and contracts at the same time. He had always been far from uncritical of the defects and wrongs of the British Empire, but held a firm belief in what it should and might be. In his later phase England, and a particular corner of England, becomes the centre of his vision. He is more concerned with the problem of the soundness of the *core* of empire; this core is something older, more natural and more permanent. But at the same time his vision takes a larger view, and he sees the Roman Empire and the place of England in it. The vision is almost that of an idea of empire laid up in heaven. And with all his geographical and historical imagination, no-one was farther than he from interest in men in the mass, or the manipulation of men in the mass: his symbol was always a particular individual. The symbol had been, at one time,

27

such men as Mulvaney or Strickland: it became Parnesius and Hobden. Technical mechanics do not lose their charm for him; wireless and aviation succeed steam, and in one of his most other-worldly stories—*They*—a considerable part is played by an early, and not very reliable, model of a motor-car: but Parnesius and Hobden are more important than the machines. One is the defender of a civilisation (of a civilisation, not of civilisation in the abstract) against barbarism; the other represents the essential contact of the civilisation with the soil.

I have said that there is always something alien about Kipling, as of a visitor from another planet; and to some readers he may still seem alien in his identification of himself with Sussex. There is an element of *tour de force* in all his work, which makes some readers uncomfortable: we are always suspicious of people who are too clever. Kipling is apt to arouse some of the same distrust as another great man who was alien in a very different way, and on a more worldly level—though he too had his vision of empire and his flashes of profound insight. Even those who admire Disraeli most may find themselves more at ease with Gladstone, whether they like the man and his politics or not. But Disraeli's foreignness was a comparatively simple matter. And undoubtedly the difference of early environment to which Kipling's foreignness is due gave him an understanding of the English countryside different from the understanding of a man born and brought up in it, and provoked in him thoughts about it which the natives would do well to heed.

It may well be unfortunate for a man's reputation that he should have great success early in life, with one work or with one type of work: for then his early work is what he is remembered by, and people (critics, sometimes, most of all) do not bother to revise their opinions in accordance with his later work. With Kipling, furthermore, a prejudice against the content may combine with a lack of understanding of the form to produce an inconsistent condemnation. On the ground of content, he is called a Tory; and on the ground of style, he is called a journalist. Neither of these terms, to be sure, need be held in anything but honour: but the former has come to acquire popular odium by a vulgar identification with a nastier name: to many people a critical attitude towards 'democracy' has come to imply a friendly attitude towards fascism—which, from a truly Tory point of view, is merely the extreme degradation of democracy. Similarly the term 'journalist', when applied to anyone not on the staff of a newspaper, has come to connote truckling to the popular taste of the moment. Kipling was not even a Tory, in the sense of one giving unquestioning loyalty to a political party: he can be called a Tory in a sense in which only a handful of writers together with a number of mostly inarticulate, obscure and uninfluential people are ever Tories in one generation. And as for being a journalist (in the sense mentioned above) we must keep in mind that the causes he espoused were not popular causes when he voiced them; that he did not aim to idealise either border warfare or the professional soldier; that his reflections on the Boer War are more admonitory than laudatory. It may be proposed that, as he dwelt upon the glory of empire, in so doing he helped to conceal its more seamy side: the commercialism, exploitation and neglect. No attentive reader of Kipling can maintain, however, that he was unaware of the faults of British rule: it is simply that he believed the British Empire to be a good thing, that he wished to set before his readers an ideal of what it should be, but was acutely aware of the difficulty of even approximating to this ideal, and of the perpetual danger of falling away even from such standard as might be attained. I cannot find any justification for the charge that he held a doctrine of race superiority. He believed that the British have a greater aptitude for ruling than other people, and that they include a greater number of kindly, incorruptible and unselfseeking men capable of administration; and he knew that scepticism in this matter is less likely to lead to greater magnanimity than it is to lead to a relaxation of the sense of responsibility. But he cannot be accused of holding that any Briton, simply because of his British race, is necessarily in any way the superior or even the equal of an individual of another race. The types of men which he admires are unlimited by any prejudice; his maturest work on India, and his greatest book, is *Kim*.

The notion of Kipling as a popular entertainer is due to the fact that his works have been popular and that they entertain. However, it is permitted to express popular views of the moment in an unpopular style: it is not approved when a man holds unpopular views and expresses them in something very readable. I do not wish to argue longer over Kipling's early 'imperialism', because there is need to speak of the development of his views. It should be said at this point, before passing on, that Kipling is not a doctrinaire or a man with a programme. His opinions are not to be considered as the antithesis of those of Mr. H. G. Wells. Mr. Wells's imagination is one thing and his political opinions another: the latter change but do not mature. But Kipling did not, in the sense in which that activity can be ascribed to Mr. Wells, think: his aim, and his gift, is to make people see—for the first condition of right thought is right sensation—the first condition of understanding a foreign country is to smell it, as you smell India in *Kim*. If you have seen and felt truly, then if God has given you the power you may be able to think rightly.

The simplest summary of the change in Kipling, in his middle years, is ' the development of the imperial imagination into the historical imagination '. To this development his settling in Sussex must have contributed to no small degree: for he had both the humility to subdue himself to his surroundings, and the freshness of the vision of stranger. My references here will be to stories rather than to poems: that is because the later unit is a poem and a story together—or a story and two poems—combining to make a form which no-one has used in the same way and in which no-one is ever likely to excel him. When I speak of 'historical imagination' I do not assume that there is only one kind. Two different kinds are exemplified by Victor Hugo and Stendhal in their accounts of the battle of Waterloo. For the first it is the charge of the Old Guard, and the sunken road of Ohain; for the latter it is Fabrice's sudden awareness that the little pattering noise around him is caused by bullets. The historian of one kind is he who gives life to abstractions; the historian of another kind may imply a whole civilisation in the behaviour of a single individual. Mr. Wells can give an epic grandeur to the accumulation of an American fortune; Mr. Lytton Strachey (to name a lesser figure) gave reality to the great by dilating upon their foibles. Kipling's imagination dwells on the particular experience of the particular man, just as his India was realised in particular men. In *The Finest Story in the World* there appears the same passion for the exact detail that is given scope in his studies of machinery. The Greek galley is described from the point of view of the galley slave. The ship was 'the kind rowed with oars, and the sea spurts through the oar-holes, and the men row sitting up to their knees in water. Then there's a bench running down between the two lines of oars, and an overseer with a whip walks up and down the bench to make the men work. . . . There's a rope running overhead, looped to the upper deck, for the overseer to catch hold of when the ship rolls. When the overseer misses the rope once and falls among the rowers, remember the hero laughs at him and gets licked for it. He's chained to his oar, of course—the hero . . . with an iron band round his waist fixed to the bench he sits on, and a sort of handcuff on his left wrist chaining him to the oar. He's on the lower deck where the worst men are sent, and the only light comes from the hatchways and through the oar-holes. Can't you imagine the sunlight just squeezing through between the handle and the hole and wobbling about as the ship moves?'

The historical imagination may give us an awful awareness of the extent of time, or it may give us a dizzy sense of the nearness of the past. It may do both. Kipling, especially in *Puck of Pook's Hill* and *Rewards and Fairies*, aims I think to give at once a sense of the antiquity of England, of the number of generations and peoples who have laboured the soil and in turn been buried beneath it, and of the contemporaneity of the past. Having previously exhibited an imaginative grasp of space, and England in it, he now proceeds to a similar achievement in time. The tales of English history need to be considered in relation to the later stories of contemporary Sussex, such as *An Habitation Enforced*, *My Son's Wife*, and *The Wish House*, together with *They* in one aspect of this curious story. Kipling's awareness and love of Sussex is a very different affair from the feeling of any other 'regional' writer of comparable fame, such as Thomas Hardy. It is not merely that he was highly conscious of what ought to be preserved, where Hardy is the chronicler of decay: or that he wrote of the Sussex which he found, where Hardy wrote of the Dorset that was already passing in his boyhood. It is, first, that the conscience of the 'fabulist' and the consciousness of the political and historical imagination are always at work. To think of Kipling as a writer who could turn his hand to any subject, who wrote of Sussex because he had exhausted his foreign and imperial material, or had satiated the public demand for it, or merely because he was a chameleon who took his colour from environment, would be to miss the mark completely: this later work is the continuation and consummation of the earlier. The second peculiarity of Kipling's Sussex stories I have already touched upon, the fact that he brings to his work the freshness of a mind and a sensibility developed and matured in quite different environment: he is discovering and reclaiming a lost inheritance. The American Chapins, in *A Habitation Enforced*, have a passive role: the protagonist in the story is the house and the life that it implies, with the profound implication that the countryman belongs to the land, the landlord to his tenants, the farmer to his labourers and not the other way about. This is a deliberate reversal of the values of industrial society. The Chapins, indeed (except for the point of their coming from a country of industrialised mentality) are a kind of mask for Kipling himself. He is also behind the hero of a less successful story in the same group, *My Son's Wife*. (I call this story less successful because he seems to point his moral a little too directly, and because the contrast between the garrulous society of London—or suburban—intellectuals and the speechless solicitor's daughter who likes hunting is hammered with too great insistence. The contrast between a bucolic world in which the second rate still participates in the good, and an intellectual world in which the second rate is usually sham and always tiresome, is not quite fair. The animus which he displays against the latter suggests that he did not have his eye on the object: for we can judge only what we understand, and must constantly dine with the opposition.) What is most important in these stories, and in *The Wish House*, and in *Friendly Brook*, is Kipling's vision of the people of the soil. It is not a Christian vision, but it is at least a pagan vision—a contradiction of the materialistic view: it is the insight into a harmony with nature which must be re-established if the truly Christian imagination is to be recovered by Christians. What he is trying to convey is, again, not a programme of agrarian reform, but a point of view unintelligible to the industrialised mind. Hence the artistic value of the *obviously*

33

incredible element of the supernatural in *The Wish House* which is exquisitely combined with the sordid realism of the women of the dialogue, the country bus, the suburban villa, and the cancer of the poor.

This hard and obscure story has to be studied in relation to the two hard and obscure poems (not here included) which precede and follow it, and which would be still more hard and obscure without the story. We have gone a long way, at this stage, from the mere story teller: a long way even from the man who felt it his duty to try to make certain things plain to his countrymen who would not see them. He could hardly have thought that many people in his own time or at any time would take the trouble to understand the parables, or even to appreciate the precision of observation, the calculating pains in selecting and combining elements, the choice of word and phrase, that were spent in their elaboration. He must have known that his own fame would get in the way, his reputation as a story teller, his reputation as a 'Tory journalist', his reputation as a facile writer who could dash off something about what happened yesterday, his reputation even as a writer of books for children which children liked to read and hear.

I return to the beginning. The late poems like the late stories with which they belong, are sometimes more obscure, because they are trying to express something more difficult than the early poems. They are the poems of a wiser and more mature writer. But they do not show any movement from 'verse' to 'poetry': they are just as instrumental as the early work, but now instruments for a matured purpose. Kipling could handle, from the beginning to the end, a considerable variety of metres and stanza forms with perfect competence; he introduces remarkable variations of his own; but as a poet he does not revolutionize. He is not one of those writers of whom one can say, that the

34

form of English poetry will always be different from what it would have been if they had not written. What fundamentally differentiates his 'verse' from 'poetry' is the subordination of musical interest. Many of the poems give, indeed, judged by the ear, an impression of the mood, some are distinctly onomatopoeic: but there is a harmonics of poetry which is not merely beyond their range—it would interfere with the intention. It is possible to argue exceptions; but I am speaking of his work as a whole, and I maintain that without understanding the purpose which animates his verse as a whole, one is not prepared to understand the exceptions.

I make no apology for having used the terms 'verse' and 'poetry' in a loose way: so that while I speak of Kipling's work as verse and not as poetry, I am still able to speak of individual compositions as poems, and also to maintain that there is 'poetry' in the 'verse'. Where terminology is loose, where we have not the vocabulary for distinctions which we feel, our only precision is found in being aware of the imperfection of our tools, and of the different senses in which we are using the same words. It should be clear that when I contrast 'verse' with 'poetry' I am not, *in this context*, implying a value judgement. I do not mean, here, by verse, the work of a man who would write poetry if he could: I mean by it something which does what 'poetry' could not do. The difference which would turn Kipling's verse into poetry, does not represent a failure or deficiency: he knew perfectly well what he was doing; and from his point of view more 'poetry' would interfere with his purpose. And I make the claim, that in speaking of Kipling we are entitled to say '*great* verse'. What other famous poets should be put into the category of great verse writers is a question which I do not here attempt to answer. That question is complicated by the fact that we should be dealing with matters as imprecise as the shape and size of a cloud or the beginning and end of

35

a wave. But the writer whose work is *always* clearly verse, is not a great verse writer: if a writer is to be that, there must be some of his work of which we cannot say whether it is verse or poetry. And the poet who could not write 'verse' when verse was needed, would be without that sense of structure which is required to make a poem of any length readable. I would suggest also that we too easily assume that what is most valuable is also most rare, and vice versa. I can think of a number of poets who have written great poetry, only of a very few whom I should call great verse writers. And unless I am mistaken, Kipling's position in this class is not only high, but unique.

Such reflections could be pursued indefinitely: but this essay is intended as an introduction: if it assists the reader to approach Kipling's verse with a fresh mind, and to regard it in a new light, and to read it as if for the first time, it will have served its purpose.

T. S. ELIOT

26th September 1941.

CONTENTS

L'Envoi (*Departmental Ditties*)   *page* 43
Dedication from *Barrack-Room Ballads*   44
Sestina of the Tramp-Royal, 1896   45
The Greek National Anthem, 1918   47
The Broken Men—1902   48
Gethsemane—1914–18   50
The Song of the Banjo, 1894   51
The Pro-Consuls   55
McAndrew's Hymn, 1893   57
The 'Mary Gloster', 1894   66
The Ballad of the 'Bolivar', 1890   76
A Song in Storm, 1914–18   78
The Last Chantey, 1892   80
The Long Trail   82
Ave Imperatrix!   86
A Song of the English, 1893   87
The Gipsy Trail   98
Our Lady of the Snows, 1897   100
The Irish Guards, 1918   102
The Settler, 1903   103
Sussex, 1902   105
The Vampire, 1897   108
When Earth's Last Picture is Painted, 1892   110
The Ballad of East and West, 1889   111
Gehazi, 1915   116

Et Dona Ferentes, 1896   *page* 118
The Holy War, 1917   120
France, 1913   122
The Bell Buoy, 1896   124
Mesopotamia, 1917   127
The Islanders, 1902   128
The Veterans   132
The Dykes, 1902   133
The White Man's Burden, 1899   136
Hymn Before Action, 1896   138
Recessional, 1897   139
'For All We Have and Are', 1914   140
The Benefactors   142
The Craftsman   143
Samuel Pepys, 1933   145
'When 'Omer Smote 'Is Bloomin' Lyre'   146
Tomlinson, 1891   146
The Last Rhyme of True Thomas, 1893   153
The Sons of Martha, 1907   159
Epitaphs of the War, 1914–18   161
'Bobs', 1898   168
Danny Deever   170
Tommy   172
'Fuzzy-Wuzzy'   174
Screw-Guns   176
Gunga Din   179
The Widow at Windsor   181
Belts   183
The Young British Soldier   185
Mandalay   187
Troopin'   190
The Widow's Party   191
Gentlemen-Rankers   193
Private Ortheris's Song   195
Shillin' a Day   196
'Back to the Army Again'   197

'Birds of Prey' March *page* 200
'Soldier an' Sailor Too' 202
Sappers 205
That Day 207
'The Men That Fought at Minden' 209
The Ladies 211
'Follow Me 'Ome' 213
The Sergeant's Weddin' 214
The 'Eathen 216
'For to Admire' 220
The Absent-Minded Beggar 222
Chant-Pagan 224
Boots 227
The Married Man 228
Stellenbosch 230
Piet 232
Ubique 235
The Return 237
'Cities and Thrones and Powers' 239
The Recall 240
Puck's Song 241
The Way Through the Woods 242
A Three-Part Song 243
The Run of the Downs 244
Sir Richard's Song (A.D. 1066) 245
A Tree Song (A.D. 1200) 246
A Charm 248
Chapter Headings 249
Cold Iron 255
'My New-Cut Ashlar' 256
'Non Nobis Domine!' 257
The Waster, 1930 258
Harp Song of the Dane Women 259
A St. Helena Lullaby 260
Road-Song of the *Bandar-Log* 262
A British-Roman Song (A.D. 406) 263

A Pict Song   *page* 264
The Law of the Jungle   265
MacDonough's Song   268
The Heritage   269
Song of the Fifth River   270
The Children's Song   272
If——   273
A Translation   274
The Land   275
The Queen's Men   279
Mine Sweepers, 1914–18   280
The Love Song of Har Dyal   281
Mowgli's Song Against People   281
'The Trade', 1914–18   282
The Runes on Weland's Sword, 1906   283
Song of the Galley-Slaves   285
The Roman Centurion's Song   285
Dane-Geld (A.D. 980–1016)   287
Norman and Saxon (A.D. 1100)   288
Edgehill Fight   290
The Dutch in the Medway (1664–72)   291
The Secret of the Machines   293
Gertrude's Prayer   294
The Gods of the Copybook Headings, 1919   295
The Storm Cone, 1932   298
The Appeal   299

A Choice of
KIPLING'S VERSE
made by T. S. Eliot

L'ENVOI

(*Departmental Ditties*)

The smoke upon your Altar dies,
  The flowers decay,
The Goddess of your sacrifice
  Has flown away.
What profit then to sing or slay
The sacrifice from day to day?

' We know the Shrine is void,' they said,
  ' The Goddess flown—
' Yet wreaths are on the altar laid—
  ' The Altar-Stone
' Is black with fumes of sacrifice,
' Albeit She has fled our eyes.

' For, it may be, if still we sing
  ' And tend the Shrine,
' Some Deity on wandering wing
  ' May there incline;
' And, finding all in order meet,
' Stay while we worship at Her feet.'

DEDICATION FROM 'BARRACK-ROOM BALLADS'

Beyond the path of the outmost sun through utter
darkness hurled—
Farther than ever comet flared or vagrant star-dust
swirled—
Live such as fought and sailed and ruled and loved and
made our world.

They are purged of pride because they died; they know
the worth of their bays;
They sit at wine with the Maidens Nine and the Gods of
the Elder Days—
It is their will to serve or be still as fitteth Our Father's
praise.

'Tis theirs to sweep through the ringing deep where
Azrael's outposts are,
Or buffet a path through the Pit's red wrath when God
goes out to war,
Or hang with the reckless Seraphim on the rein of a red-
maned star.

They take their mirth in the joy of the Earth—they dare
not grieve for her pain.
They know of toil and the end of toil; they know God's
Law is plain;
So they whistle the Devil to make them sport who know
that Sin is vain.

And oft-times cometh our wise Lord God, master of every
trade,
And tells them tales of His daily toil, of Edens newly
made;
And they rise to their feet as He passes by, gentlemen
unafraid.

To these who are cleansed of base Desire, Sorrow and
     Lust and Shame—
Gods for they knew the hearts of men, men for they
     stooped to Fame—
Borne on the breath that men call Death, my brother's
     spirit came.

He scarce had need to doff his pride or slough the dross
     of Earth—
E'en as he trod that day to God so walked he from his
     birth,
In simpleness and gentleness and honour and clean mirth.

So cup to lip in fellowship they gave him welcome high
And made him place at the banquet board—the Strong
     Men ranged thereby,
Who had done his work and held his peace and had no
     fear to die.

Beyond the loom of the last lone star, through open dark-
     ness hurled,
Further than rebel comet dared or hiving star-swarm
     swirled,
Sits he with those that praise our God for that they served
     His world.

SESTINA OF THE TRAMP-ROYAL
1896

Speakin' in general, I 'ave tried 'em all—
  The 'appy roads that take you o'er the world.
Speakin' in general, I 'ave found them good
For such as cannot use one bed too long,
But must get 'ence, the same as I 'ave done,
An' go observin' matters till they die.

What do it matter where or 'ow we die,
So long as we've our 'ealth to watch it all—
The different ways that different things are done,
An' men an' women lovin' in this world;
Takin' our chances as they come along,
An' when they ain't, pretendin' they are good?

In cash or credit—no, it aren't no good;
You 'ave to 'ave the 'abit or you'd die,
Unless you lived your life but one day long,
Nor didn't prophesy nor fret at all,
But drew your tucker some'ow from the world,
An' never bothered what you might ha' done.

But, Gawd, what things are they I 'aven't done?
I've turned my 'and to most, an' turned it good,
In various situations round the world—
For 'im that doth not work must surely die;
But that's no reason man should labour all
'Is life on one same shift—life's none so long.

Therefore, from job to job I've moved along.
Pay couldn't 'old me when my time was done,
For something in my 'ead upset it all,
Till I 'ad dropped whatever 'twas for good,
An', out at sea, be'eld the dock-lights die,
An' met my mate—the wind that tramps the world!

It's like a book, I think, this bloomin' world,
Which you can read and care for just so long,
But presently you feel that you will die
Unless you get the page you're readin' done,
An' turn another—likely not so good;
But what you're after is to turn 'em all.

Gawd bless this world!   Whatever she 'ath done—
Excep' when awful long—I've found it good.
So write, before I die, "E liked it all!"

THE GREEK NATIONAL ANTHEM
1918

We knew thee of old,
  Oh, divinely restored,
By the light of thine eyes
  And the light of thy Sword.

From the graves of our slain
  Shall thy valour prevail
As we greet thee again—
  Hail, Liberty!   Hail!

Long time didst thou dwell
  Mid the peoples that mourn,
Awaiting some voice
  That should bid thee return.

Ah, slow broke that day
  And no man dared call,
For the shadow of tyranny
  Lay over all:

And we saw thee sad-eyed,
  The tears on thy cheeks
While thy raiment was dyed
  In the blood of the Greeks.

Yet, behold now thy sons
  With impetuous breath
Go forth to the fight
  Seeking Freedom or Death.

From the graves of our slain
  Shall thy valour prevail
As we greet thee again—
  Hail, Liberty! Hail!

THE BROKEN MEN
1902

For things we never mention,
  For Art misunderstood—
For excellent intention
  That did not turn to good;
From ancient tales' renewing,
  From clouds we would not clear—
Beyond the Law's pursuing
  We fled, and settled here.

We took no tearful leaving,
  We bade no long good-byes.
Men talked of crime and thieving,
  Men wrote of fraud and lies.
To save our injured feelings
  'Twas time and time to go—
Behind was dock and Dartmoor,
  Ahead lay Callao!

The widow and the orphan
  That pray for ten per cent,

They clapped their trailers on us
    To spy the road we went.
They watched the foreign sailings
    (They scan the shipping still),
And that's your Christian people
    Returning good for ill!

God bless the thoughtful islands
    Where never warrants come;
God bless the just Republics
    That give a man a home,
That ask no foolish questions,
    But set him on his feet;
And save his wife and daughters
    From the workhouse and the street.

On church and square and market
    The noonday silence falls;
You'll hear the drowsy mutter
    Of the fountain in our halls.
Asleep amid the yuccas
    The city takes her ease—
Till twilight brings the land-wind
    To the clicking jalousies.

Day long the diamond weather,
    The high, unaltered blue—
The smell of goats and incense
    And the mule-bells tinkling through.
Day long the warder ocean
    That keeps us from our kin,
And once a month our levée
    When the English mail comes in.

You'll find us up and waiting
    To treat you at the bar;

You'll find us less exclusive
    Than the average English are.
We'll meet you with a carriage,
    Too glad to show you round,
But—we do not lunch on steamers,
    For they are English ground.

We sail o' nights to England
    And join our smiling Boards—
Our wives go in with Viscounts
    And our daughters dance with Lords,
But behind our princely doings,
    And behind each coup we make,
We feel there's Something Waiting,
    And—we meet It when we wake.

Ah, God! One sniff of England—
    To greet our flesh and blood—
To hear the traffic slurring
    Once more through London mud!
Our towns of wasted honour—
    Our streets of lost delight!
How stands the old Lord Warden?
    Are Dover's cliffs still white?

GETHSEMANE

1914–18

The Garden called Gethsemane
    In Picardy it was,
And there the people came to see
    The English soldiers pass.
We used to pass—we used to pass
    Or halt, as it might be.

And ship our masks in case of gas
    Beyond Gethsemane.

The Garden called Gethsemane,
    It held a pretty lass,
But all the time she talked to me
    I prayed my cup might pass.
The officer sat on the chair,
    The men lay on the grass,
And all the time we halted there
    I prayed my cup might pass.

It didn't pass—it didn't pass—
    It didn't pass from me.
I drank it when we met the gas
    Beyond Gethsemane!

THE SONG OF THE BANJO
1894

You couldn't pack a Broadwood half a mile—
    You mustn't leave a fiddle in the damp—
You couldn't raft an organ up the Nile,
    And play it in an Equatorial swamp.
I travel with the cooking-pots and pails—
    I'm sandwiched 'tween the coffee and the pork—
And when the dusty column checks and tails,
    You should hear me spur the rearguard to a walk!

With my '*Pilly-willy-winky-winky-popp!*'
    [Oh, it's any tune that comes into my head!]
So I keep 'em moving forward till they drop;
    So I play 'em up to water and to bed.

In the silence of the camp before the fight,
  When it's good to make your will and say your prayer,
You can hear my *strumpty-tumpty* overnight,
  Explaining ten to one was always fair.
I'm the Prophet of the Utterly Absurd,
  Of the Patently Impossible and Vain—
And when the Thing that Couldn't has occurred,
  Give me time to change my leg and go again.

    With my '*Tumpa-tumpa-tumpa-tumpa-tump!*'
      In the desert where the dung-fed camp-smoke
        curled.
    There was never voice before us till I led our lonely
        chorus,
      I—the war-drum of the White Man round the
        world!

By the bitter road the Younger Son must tread,
  Ere he win to hearth and saddle of his own,—
'Mid the riot of the shearers at the shed,
  In the silence of the herder's hut alone—
In the twilight, on a bucket upside down,
  Hear me babble what the weakest won't confess—
I am Memory and Torment—I am Town!
  I am all that ever went with evening dress!

    With my '*Tunka-tunka-tunka-tunka-tunk!*'
      [So the lights—the London Lights—grow near and
        plain!]
    So I rowel 'em afresh towards the Devil and the Flesh
      Till I bring my broken rankers home again.

In desire of many marvels over sea,
  Where the new-raised tropic city sweats and roars,
I have sailed with Young Ulysses from the quay
  Till the anchor rumbled down on stranger shores.

He is blooded to the open and the sky,
    He is taken in a snare that shall not fail,
He shall hear me singing strongly, till he die,
    Like the shouting of a backstay in a gale.

      With my '*Hya! Heeya! Heeya! Hullah! Haul!*'
        [Oh, the green that thunders aft along the deck!]
      Are you sick o' towns and men? You must sign and
          sail again,
        For it's 'Johnny Bowlegs, pack your kit and
          trek!'

Through the gorge that gives the stars at noon-day clear—
    Up the pass that packs the scud beneath our wheel—
Round the bluff that sinks her thousand fathom sheer—
    Down the valley with our guttering brakes asqueal:
Where the trestle groans and quivers in the snow,
    Where the many-shedded levels loop and twine,
Hear me lead my reckless children from below
    Till we sing the Song of Roland to the pine!

      With my '*Tinka-tinka-tinka-tinka-tink!*'
        [Oh, the axe has cleared the mountain, croup and
          crest!]
      And we ride the iron stallions down to drink,
        Through the cañons to the waters of the West!

And the tunes that mean so much to you alone—
    Common tunes that make you choke and blow your
      nose—
Vulgar tunes that bring the laugh that brings the groan—
    I can rip your very heartstrings out with those;
With the feasting, and the folly, and the fun—
    And the lying, and the lusting, and the drink,
And the merry play that drops you, when you're done,
    To the thoughts that burn like irons if you think.

With my '*Plunka-lunka-lunka-lunka-lunk!*'
  Here's a trifle on account of pleasure past,
Ere the wit that made you win gives you eyes to see
      your sin
    And—the heavier repentance at the last!

Let the organ moan her sorrow to the roof—
  I have told the naked stars the Grief of Man!
Let the trumpet snare the foeman to the proof—
  I have known Defeat, and mocked it as we ran!
My bray ye may not alter nor mistake
  When I stand to jeer the fatted Soul of Things,
But the Song of Lost Endeavour that I make,
  Is it hidden in the twanging of the strings?

  With my '*Ta-ra-rara-rara-ra-ra-rrrp!*'
    [Is it naught to you that hear and pass me by?]
  But the word—the word is mine, when the order
      moves the line
    And the lean, locked ranks go roaring down to die!

The grandam of my grandam was the Lyre—
  [Oh, the blue below the little fisher-huts!]
That the Stealer stooping beachward filled with fire,
  Till she bore my iron head and ringing guts!
By the wisdom of the centuries I speak—
  To the tune of yestermorn I set the truth—
I, the joy of life unquestioned—I, the Greek—
  I, the everlasting Wonder-song of Youth!

  With my '*Tinka-tinka-tinka-tinka-tink!*'
    [What d'ye lack, my noble masters! What d'ye
      lack?]
  So I draw the world together link by link :
    Yea, from Delos up to Limerick and back!

THE PRO-CONSULS

(LORD MILNER)

The overfaithful sword returns the user
His heart's desire at price of his heart's blood.
The clamour of the arrogant accuser
Wastes that one hour we needed to make good.
This was foretold of old at our outgoing;
This we accepted who have squandered, knowing,
The strength and glory of our reputations,
At the day's need, as it were dross, to guard
The tender and new-dedicate foundations
Against the sea we fear—not man's award.

They that dig foundations deep,
    Fit for realms to rise upon,
Little honour do they reap
    Of their generation,
Any more than mountains gain
Stature till we reach the plain.

With no veil before their face
    Such as shroud or sceptre lend—
Daily in the market-place,
    Of one height to foe and friend—
They must cheapen self to find
Ends uncheapened for mankind.

Through the night when hirelings rest,
    Sleepless they arise, alone,
The unsleeping arch to test
    And the o'er-trusted corner-stone,
'Gainst the need, they know, that lies
Hid behind the centuries.

Not by lust of praise or show,
　　Not by Peace herself betrayed—
Peace herself must they forgo
　　Till that peace be fitly made;
And in single strength uphold
Wearier hands and hearts acold.

On the stage their act hath framed
　　For thy sports, O Liberty!
Doubted are they, and defamed
　　By the tongues their act set free,
While they quicken, tend and raise
Power that must their power displace.

Lesser men feign greater goals,
　　Failing whereof they may sit
Scholarly to judge the souls
　　That go down into the Pit
And, despite its certain clay,
Heave a new world toward the day.

These at labour make no sign,
　　More than planets, tides or years
Which discover God's design,
　　Not our hopes and not our fears;
Nor in aught they gain or lose
Seek a triumph or excuse!

For, so the Ark be borne to Zion, who
Heeds how they perished or were paid that bore it?
For, so the Shrine abide, what shame—what pride—
If we, the priests, were bound or crowned before it?

McANDREW'S HYMN

1893

Lord, Thou hast made this world below the shadow of
a dream,
An', taught by time, I tak' it so—exceptin' always Steam.
From coupler-flange to spindle-guide I see Thy Hand, O
God—
Predestination in the stride o' yon connectin'-rod.
John Calvin might ha' forged the same—enorrmous, cer-
tain, slow—
Ay, wrought it in the furnace-flame—*my* 'Institutio.'
I cannot get my sleep to-night; old bones are hard to
please;
I'll stand the middle watch up here—alone wi' God an'
these
My engines, after ninety days o' race an' rack an' strain
Through all the seas of all Thy world, slam-bangin' home
again.
Slam-bang too much—they knock a wee—the crosshead-
gibs are loose,
But thirty thousand mile o' sea has gied them fair ex-
cuse. . . .
Fine, clear an' dark—a full-draught breeze, wi' Ushant out
o' sight,
An' Ferguson relievin' Hay. Old girl, ye'll walk to-night!
His wife's at Plymouth. . . . Seventy—One—Two—
Three since he began—
Three turns for Mistress Ferguson . . . and who's to
blame the man?
There's none at any port for me, by drivin' fast or slow,
Since Elsie Campbell went to Thee, Lord, thirty years ago
(The year the *Sarah Sands* was burned. Oh, roads we used
to tread,
Fra' Maryhill to Pollokshaws—fra' Govan to Parkhead!)

Not but they're ceevil on the Board. Ye'll hear Sir Ken-
neth say :
'Good morrn, McAndrew! Back again? An' how's your
bilge to-day?'
Miscallin' technicalities but handin' me my chair
To drink Madeira wi' three Earls—the auld Fleet Engineer
That started as a boiler-whelp—when steam and he were
low.
I mind the time we used to serve a broken pipe wi' tow!
Ten pound was all the pressure then—Eh! Eh!—a man
wad drive;
An' here, our workin' gauges give one hunder sixty-five!
We're creepin' on wi' each new rig—less weight an' larger
power;
There'll be the loco-boiler next an' thirty mile an hour!
Thirty an' more. What I ha' seen since ocean-steam began
Leaves me na doot for the machine: but what about the
man?
The man that counts, wi' all his runs, one million mile o'
sea :
Four time the span from earth to moon. . . . How far,
O Lord, from Thee
That wast beside him night an' day? Ye mind my first
typhoon?
It scoughed the skipper on his way to jock wi' the saloon.
Three feet were on the stokehold-floor—just slappin' to
an' fro—
An' cast me on a furnace-door. I have the marks to
show.
Marks! I ha' marks o' more than burns—deep in my soul
an' black,
An' times like this, when things go smooth, my wickud-
ness comes back.
The sins o' four an' forty years, all up an' down the seas,
Clack an' repeat like valves half-fed. . . . Forgie 's our
trespasses!

Nights when I'd come on deck to mark, wi' envy in my
  gaze,
The couples kittlin' in the dark between the funnel-
  stays;
Years when I raked the Ports wi' pride to fill my cup o'
  wrong—
Judge not, O Lord, my steps aside at Gay Street in Hong-
  Kong!
Blot out the wastrel hours of mine in sin when I abode—
Jane Harrigan's an' Number Nine, The Reddick an' Grant
  Road!
An' waur than all—my crownin' sin—rank blasphemy an'
  wild.
I was not four and twenty then—Ye wadna judge a
  child?
I'd seen the Tropics first that run—new fruit, new smells,
  new air—
How could I tell—blind-fou wi' sun—the Deil was lurkin'
  there?
By day like playhouse-scenes the shore slid past our sleepy
  eyes;
By night those soft, lasceevious stars leered from those
  velvct skies,
In port (we used no cargo-steam) I'd daunder down the
  streets—
An ijjit grinnin' in a dream—for shells an' parrakeets,
An' walkin'-sticks o' carved bamboo an' blowfish stuffed
  an' dried—
Fillin' my bunk wi' rubbishry the Chief put overside.
Till, off Sambawa Head, Ye mind, I heard a land-breeze
  ca',
Milk-warm wi' breath o' spice an' bloom: 'McAndrew,
  come awa'!'
Firm, clear an' low—no haste, no hate—the ghostly
  whisper went,
Just statin' eevidential facts beyon' all argument:

59

'Your mither's God's a graspin' deil, the shadow o'
    yoursel',
'Got out o' books by meenisters clean daft on Heaven an'
    Hell.
'They mak' him in the Broomielaw, o' Glasgie cold an'
    dirt,
'A jealous, pridefu' fetich, lad, that's only strong to
    hurt.
'Ye'll not go back to Him again an' kiss His red-hot
    rod,
'But come wi' Us' (Now, who were *They*?) 'an' know
    the Leevin' God,
'That does not kipper souls for sport or break a life in
    jest,
'But swells the ripenin' cocoanuts an' ripes the woman's
    breast.'
An' there it stopped—cut off—no more—that quiet, cer-
    tain voice—
For me, six months o' twenty-four, to leave or take at
    choice.
'Twas on me like a thunderclap—it racked me through an'
    through—
Temptation past the show o' speech, unnameable an'
    new —
The Sin against the Holy Ghost? . . . An' under all,
    our screw.

That storm blew by but left behind her anchor-shiftin'
    swell.
Thou knowest all my heart an' mind, Thou knowest, Lord,
    I fell—
Third on the *Mary Gloster* then, and first that night in
    Hell!
Yet was Thy Hand beneath my head, about my feet Thy
    Care—
Fra' Deli clear to Torres Strait, the trial o' despair,

But when we touched the Barrier Reef Thy answer to my
        prayer! . . .
We dared na run that sea by night but lay an' held
        our fire,
An' I was drowsin' on the hatch—sick—sick wi' doubt an'
        tire :
'*Better the sight of eyes that see than wanderin' o' desire!*'
Ye mind that word? Clear as our gongs—again, an' once
        again,
When rippin' down through coral-trash ran out our
        moorin'-chain :
An', by Thy Grace, I had the Light to see my duty plain.
Light on the engine-room—no more—bright as our
        carbons burn.
I've lost it since a thousand times, but never past return!

.   .   .   .   .

Obsairve! Per annum we'll have here two thousand souls
        aboard—
Think not I dare to justify myself before the Lord,
But—average fifteen hunder souls safe-borne fra' port to
        port—
I *am* o' service to my kind. Ye wadna blame the thought?
Maybe they steam from Grace to Wrath—to sin by folly
        led—
It isna mine to judge their path—their lives are on my
        head.
Mine at the last—when all is done it all comes back to me,
The fault that leaves six thousand ton a log upon the sea.
We'll tak' one stretch—three weeks an' odd by ony road
        ye steer—
Fra' Cape Town east to Wellington—ye need an engineer.
Fail there—ye've time to weld your shaft—ay, eat it, ere
        ye're spoke ;
Or make Kerguelen under sail—three jiggers burned wi'
        smoke!

An' home again—the Rio run: it's no child's play to go
Steamin' to bell for fourteen days o' snow an' floe an'
    blow.
The bergs like kelpies overside that girn an' turn an' shift
Whaur, grindin' like the Mills o' God, goes by the big
    South drift.
(Hail, Snow and Ice that praise the Lord. I've met them
    at their work,
An' wished we had anither route or they anither kirk.)
Yon's strain, hard strain, o' head an' hand, for though Thy
    Power brings
All skill to naught, Ye'll understand a man must think o'
    things.
Then, at the last, we'll get to port an' hoist their baggage
    clear—
The passengers, wi' gloves an' canes—an' this is what I'll
    hear:
'Well, thank ye for a pleasant voyage. The tender's
    comin' now.'
While I go testin' follower-bolts an' watch the skipper bow.
They've words for every one but me—shake hands wi'
    half the crew,
Except the dour Scots engineer, the man they never knew.
An' yet I like the wark for all we've dam'-few pickin's
    here—
No pension, an' the most we'll earn's four hunder pound
    a year.
Better myself abroad? Maybe. *I'd* sooner starve than sail
Wi' such as call a snifter-rod *ross* . . . French for nightin-
    gale.
Commeesion on my stores? Some do; but I cannot afford
To lie like stewards wi' patty-pans. I'm older than the
    Board.
A bonus on the coal I save? Ou ay, the Scots are close,
But when I grudge the strength Ye gave I'll grudge their
    food to *those*.

(There's bricks that I might recommend—an' clink the
    firebars cruel.
No! Welsh—Wangarti at the worst—an' damn all patent
    fuel!)
Inventions? Ye must stay in port to mak' a patent pay.
My Deeferential Valve-Gear taught me how that business
    lay.
I blame no chaps wi' clearer heads for aught they make or
    sell.
I found that I could not invent an' look to these as well.
So, wrestled wi' Apollyon—Nah!—fretted like a bairn—
But burned the workin'-plans last run, wi' all I hoped to
    earn.
Ye know how hard an Idol dies, an' what that meant to
    me—
E'en tak' it for a sacrifice acceptable to Thee. . . .
Below there! Oiler! What's your wark? Ye find it runnin'
    hard?
Ye needn't swill the cup wi' oil—this isn't the Cunard!
Ye thought? Ye are not paid to think. Go, sweat that off
    again!
Tck! Tck! It's deeficult to sweer nor tak' The Name in
    vain!
Men, ay, an' women, call me stern. Wi' these to oversee
Ye'll note I've little time to burn on social repartee.
The bairns see what their elders miss; they'll hunt me to
    an' fro,
Till for the sake of—well, a kiss—I tak' 'em down below.
That minds me of our Viscount loon—Sir Kenneth's kin—
    the chap
Wi' Russia-leather tennis-shoon an' spar-decked yachtin'-
    cap.
I showed him round last week, o'er all—an' at the last says
    he:
'Mister McAndrew, don't you think steam spoils romance
    at sea?'

Damned ijjit! I'd been doon that morn to see what ailed
the throws,
Manholin', on my back—the cranks three inches off my
nose.
Romance! Those first-class passengers they like it very
well,
Printed an' bound in little books; but why don't poets
tell?
I'm sick of all their quirks an' turns—the loves an' doves
they dream—
Lord, send a man like Robbie Burns to sing the Song o'
Steam!
To match wi' Scotia's noblest speech yon orchestra sub-
lime
Whaurto—uplifted like the Just—the tail-rods mark the
time.
The crank-throws give the double-bass, the feed-pump
sobs an' heaves,
An' now the main eccentrics start their quarrel on the
sheaves:
Her time, her own appointed time, the rocking link-head
bides,
Till—hear that note?—the rod's return whings glimmerin'
through the guides.
They're all awa'! True beat, full power, the clangin'
chorus goes
Clear to the tunnel where they sit, my purrin' dynamoes.
Interdependence absolute, foreseen, ordained, decreed,
To work, Ye'll note, at ony tilt an' every rate o'
speed.
Fra' skylight-lift to furnace-bars, backed, bolted, braced
an' stayed,
An' singin' like the Mornin' Stars for joy that they are
made;
While, out o' touch o' vanity, the sweatin' thrust-block
says:
'Not unto us the praise, or man—not unto us the praise!'

Now, a' together, hear them lift their lesson—theirs an'
  mine:
'Law, Orrder, Duty an' Restraint, Obedience, Disci-
  pline!'
Mill, forge an' try-pit taught them that when roarin' they
  arose,
An' whiles I wonder if a soul was gied them wi' the blows.
Oh for a man to weld it then, in one trip-hammer strain,
Till even first-class passengers could tell the meanin' plain!
But no one cares except mysel' that serve an' understand
My seven thousand horse-power here. Eh, Lord! They're
  grand—they're grand!
Uplift am I? When first in store the new-made beasties
  stood,
Were Ye cast down that breathed the Word declarin' all
  things good?
Not so! O' that warld-liftin' joy no after-fall culd vex,
Ye've left a glimmer still to cheer the Man—the Arrtifex!
That holds, in spite o' knock and scale, o' friction, waste
  an' slip,
An' by that light—now, mark my word—we'll build the
  Perfect Ship.
I'll never last to judge her lines or take her curve—not I.
But I ha' lived an' I ha' worked. Be thanks to Thee, Most
  High!
An' I ha' done what I ha' done—judge Thou if ill or
  well—
Always Thy Grace preventin' me. . . .
                        Losh! Yon's the 'Stand-by' bell.
Pilot so soon? His flare it is. The mornin'-watch is set.
Well, God be thanked, as I was sayin', I'm no Pelagian yet.
Now I'll tak' on. . . .
  'Morrn, Ferguson. Man, have ye ever thought
What your good leddy costs in coal? . . . I'll burn 'em
  down to port.

65

THE 'MARY GLOSTER'
1894

I've paid for your sickest fancies; I've humoured your
    crackedest whim—
Dick, it's your daddy, dying; you've got to listen to
    him!
Good for a fortnight, am I? The doctor told you? He
    lied.
I shall go under by morning, and—— Put that nurse out-
    side.
'Never seen death yet, Dickie? Well, now is your time to
    learn,
And you'll wish you held my record before it comes to
    your turn.
Not counting the Line and the Foundry, the Yards and
    the village, too,
I've made myself and a million; but I'm damned if I made
    you.
Master at two-and-twenty, and married at twenty-
    three—
Ten thousand men on the pay-roll, and forty freighters at
    sea!
Fifty years between 'em, and every year of it fight,
And now I'm Sir Anthony Gloster, dying, a baronite:
For I lunched with his Royal 'Ighness—what was it the
    papers had?
'Not least of our merchant-princes.' Dickie, that's me,
    your dad!
I didn't begin with askings. *I* took my job and I stuck;
I took the chances they wouldn't, an' now they're calling
    it luck.
Lord, what boats I've handled—rotten and leaky and old—
Ran 'em, or—opened the bilge-cock, precisely as I was
    told.

Grub that 'ud bind you crazy, and crews that 'ud turn you
  grey,
And a big fat lump of insurance to cover the risk on the
  way.
The others they dursn't do it; they said they valued their
  life
(They've served me since as skippers). *I* went, and I took
  my wife.
Over the world I drove 'em, married at twenty-
  three,
And your mother saving the money and making a man of
  me.
I was content to be master, but she said there was better
  behind;
She took the chances I wouldn't, and I followed your
  mother blind.
She egged me to borrow the money, an' she helped me to
  clear the loan,
When we bought half-shares in a cheap 'un and hoisted a
  flag of our own.
Patching and coaling on credit, and living the Lord knew
  how,
We started the Red Ox freighters—we've eight-and-thirty
  now.
And those were the days of clippers, and the freights were
  clipper-freights,
And we knew we were making our fortune, but she died in
  Macassar Straits—
By the Little Paternosters, as you come to the Union
  Bank—
And we dropped her in fourteen fathom: I pricked it off
  where she sank.
Owners we were, full owners, and the boat was christened
  for her,
And she died in the *Mary Gloster*. My heart, how young
  we were!

67

So I went on a spree round Java and wellnigh ran her
ashore,
But your mother came and warned me and I wouldn't
liquor no more:
Strict I stuck to my business, afraid to stop or I'd
think,
Saving the money (she warned me), and letting the other
men drink.
And I met M'Cullough in London (I'd saved five 'undred
then),
And 'tween us we started the Foundry—three forges and
twenty men.
Cheap repairs for the cheap 'uns. It paid, and the business
grew;
For I bought me a steam-lathe patent, and that was a gold
mine too.
'Cheaper to build 'em than buy 'em,' *I* said, but
M'Cullough he shied,
And we wasted a year in talking before we moved to the
Clyde.
And the Lines were all beginning, and we all of us started
fair,
Building our engines like houses and staying the boilers
square.
But M'Cullough 'e wanted cabins with marble and maple
and all,
And Brussels an' Utrecht velvet, and baths and a Social
Hall,
And pipes for closets all over, and cutting the frames too
light,
But M'Cullough he died in the Sixties, and—— Well, I'm
dying to-night. . . .
I knew—*I* knew what was coming, when we bid on the
Byfleet's keel—
They piddled and piffled with iron. I'd given my orders
for steel!

Steel and the first expansions. It paid, I tell you, it
  paid,
When we came with our nine-knot freighters and collared
  the long-run trade!
And they asked me how I did it, and I gave 'em the Scrip-
  ture text,
'You keep your light so shining a little in front o' the
  next!'
They copied all they could follow, but they couldn't copy
  my mind,
And I left 'em sweating and stealing a year and a half
  behind.
Then came the armour-contracts, but that was M'Cul-
  lough's side;
He was always best in the Foundry, but better, perhaps,
  he died.
I went through his private papers; the notes was plainer
  than print;
And I'm no fool to finish if a man'll give me a
  hint.
(I remember his widow was angry.) So I saw what his
  drawings meant,
And I started the six-inch rollers, and it paid me sixty per
  cent.
Sixty per cent *with* failures, and more than twice we could
  do,
And a quarter-million to credit, and I saved it all for
  you!
I thought—it doesn't matter—you seemed to favour your
  ma,
But you're nearer forty than thirty, and I know the kind
  you are.
Harrer an' Trinity College! I ought to ha' sent you to
  sea—
But I stood you an education, an' what have you done for
  me?

69

The things I knew was proper you wouldn't thank me to
give,
And the things I knew was rotten you said was the way to
live.
For you muddled with books and pictures, an' china an'
etchin's an' fans,
And your rooms at college was beastly—more like a
whore's than a man's;
Till you married that thin-flanked woman, as white and as
stale as a bone,
An' she gave you your social nonsense; but where's that
kid o' your own?
I've seen your carriages blocking the half o' the Cromwell
Road,
But never the doctor's brougham to help the missus
unload.
(So there isn't even a grandchild, an' the Gloster family's
done.)
Not like your mother, she isn't. *She* carried her freight
each run.
But they died, the pore little beggars! At sea she had 'em
—they died.
Only you, an' you stood it. You haven't stood much
beside.
Weak, a liar, and idle, and mean as a collier's
whelp
Nosing for scraps in the galley. No help—my son was no
help!
So he gets three 'undred thousand, in trust and the
interest paid.
I wouldn't give it you, Dickie—you see, I made it in
trade.
You're saved from soiling your fingers, and if you have
no child,
It all comes back to the business. 'Gad, won't your wife
be wild!

And so you'll write to McAndrew, he's Chief of the
    Maori Line;
They'll give him leave, if you ask 'em and say it's business
    o' mine.
I built three boats for the Maoris, an' very well pleased
    they were,
An' I've known Mac since the Fifties, and Mac knew me—
    and her.
After the first stroke warned me I sent him the money to
    keep
Against the time you'd claim it, committin' your dad to
    the deep;
For you are the son o' my body, and Mac was my oldest
    friend,
I've never asked 'im to dinner, but he'll see it out to the
    end.
Stiff-necked Glasgow beggar! I've heard he's prayed for
    my soul,
But he couldn't lie if you paid him, and he'd starve before
    he stole.
He'll take the *Mary* in ballast—you'll find her a lively
    ship;
And you'll take Sir Anthony Gloster, that goes on 'is
    wedding-trip,
Lashed in our old deck-cabin with all three port-holes
    wide,
The kick o' the screw beneath him and the round blue seas
    outside!
Sir Anthony Gloster's carriage—our 'ouse-flag flyin'
    free—
Ten thousand men on the pay-roll and forty freighters at
    sea!
He made himself and a million, but this world is a fleetin'
    show,
And he'll go to the wife of 'is bosom the same as he ought
    to go—

By the heel of the Paternosters—there isn't a chance to
    mistake—
And Mac'll pay you the money as soon as the bubbles
    break!
Five thousand for six weeks' cruising, the staunchest
    freighter afloat,
And Mac he'll give you your bonus the minute I'm out o'
    the boat!
He'll take you round to Macassar, and you'll come back
    alone;
He knows what I want o' the *Mary*. . . . I'll do what I
    please with my own.
Your mother 'ud call it wasteful, but I've seven-and-thirty
    more;
I'll come in my private carriage and bid it wait at the
    door. . . .
For my son 'e was never a credit: 'e muddled with books
    and art,
And 'e lived on Sir Anthony's money and 'e broke Sir
    Anthony's heart.
There isn't even a grandchild, and the Gloster family's
    done—
The only one you left me—O mother, the only one!
Harrer and Trinity College—me slavin' early an' late—
An' he thinks I'm dying crazy, and you're in Macassar
    Strait!
Flesh o' my flesh, my dearie, for ever an' ever amen,
That first stroke come for a warning. I ought to ha' gone
    to you then.
But—cheap repairs for a cheap 'un—the doctors said I'd
    do.
Mary, why didn't *you* warn me? I've allus heeded to you,
Excep'—I know—about women; but you are a spirit
    now;
An', wife, they was only women, and I was a man. That's
    how.

An' a man 'e must go with a woman, as you *could* not
understand;
But I never talked 'em secrets. I paid 'em out o' hand.
Thank Gawd, I can pay for my fancies! Now what's five
thousand to me,
For a berth off the Paternosters in the haven where I
would be?
I believe in the Resurrection, if I read my Bible plain,
But I wouldn't trust 'em at Wokin'; we're safer at sea
again.
For the heart it shall go with the treasure—go down to
the sea in ships.
I'm sick of the hired women. I'll kiss my girl on her lips!
I'll be content with my fountain. I'll drink from my own
well,
And the wife of my youth shall charm me—an' the rest
can go to Hell!
(Dickie, *he* will, that's certain.) I'll lie in our standin'-bed,
An' Mac'll take her in ballast—an' she trims best by the
head. . . .
Down by the head an' sinkin', her fires are drawn and cold,
And the water's splashin' hollow on the skin of the empty
hold—
Churning an' choking and chuckling, quiet and scummy
and dark—
Full to her lower hatches and risin' steady. Hark!
That was the after-bulkhead. . . . She's flooded from
stem to stern. . . .
'Never seen death yet, Dickie? . . . Well, now is your
time to learn!

THE BALLAD OF THE 'BOLIVAR'
1890

Seven men from all the world back to Docks again,
Rolling down the Ratcliffe Road drunk and raising
Cain.
Give the girls another drink 'fore we sign away—
We that took the Bolivar *out across the Bay!*

We put out from Sunderland loaded down with rails;
    We put back to Sunderland 'cause our cargo shifted;
We put out from Sunderland—met the winter gales—
    Seven days and seven nights to The Start we drifted.

        Racketing her rivets loose, smoke-stack white as
           snow,
        All the coals adrift adeck, half the rails below,
        Leaking like a lobster-pot, steering like a dray—
        Out we took the *Bolivar*, out across the Bay!

One by one the Lights came up, winked and let us by;
    Mile by mile we waddled on, coal and fo'c'sle short;
Met a blow that laid us down, heard a bulkhead fly;
    Left The Wolf behind us with a two-foot list to port.

        Trailing like a wounded duck, working out her
           soul;
        Clanging like a smithy-shop after every roll;
        Just a funnel and a mast lurching through the spray—
        So we threshed the *Bolivar* out across the Bay!

Felt her hog and felt her sag, betted when she'd break;
    Wondered every time she raced if she'd stand the shock;
Heard the seas like drunken men pounding at her strake;
    Hoped the Lord 'ud keep His thumb on the plummer-
        block!

Banged against the iron decks, bilges choked with
    coal;
Flayed and frozen foot and hand, sick of heart and
    soul;
'Last we prayed she'd buck herself into Judgment
    Day—
Hi! we cursed the *Bolivar* knocking round the Bay!

O her nose flung up to sky, groaning to be still—
Up and down and back we went, never time for breath;
Then the money paid at Lloyd's caught her by the keel,
And the stars ran round and round dancin' at our death!

Aching for an hour's sleep, dozing off between:
'Heard the rotten rivets draw when she took it green;
'Watched the compass chase its tail like a cat at play—
That was on the *Bolivar*, south across the Bay!

Once we saw between the squalls, lyin' head to swell—
Mad with work and weariness, wishin' they was we—
Some damned Liner's lights go by like a grand hotel;
'Cheered her from the *Bolivar* swampin' in the sea.

Then a greybeard cleared us out, then the skipper
    laughed;
'Boys, the wheel has gone to Hell—rig the winches
    aft!
'Yoke the kicking rudder-head—get her under way!'
So we steered her, pully-haul, out across the Bay!

Just a pack o' rotten plates puttied up with tar,
In we came, an' time enough, 'cross Bilbao Bar.
Overloaded, undermanned, meant to founder, we
Euchred God Almighty's storm, bluffed the Eternal Sea!

77

Seven men from all the world back to town again,
Rollin' down the Ratcliffe Road drunk and raising Cain:
Seven men from out of Hell. Ain't the owners gay,
Cause we took the Bolivar *safe across the Bay?*

A SONG IN STORM

1914–18

Be well assured that on our side
    The abiding oceans fight,
Though headlong wind and heaping tide
    Make us their sport to-night.
By force of weather, not of war,
    In jeopardy we steer:
Then welcome Fate's discourtesy
    Whereby it shall appear
      How in all time of our distress,
      And our deliverance too,
      The game is more than the player of the game,
      And the ship is more than the crew!

Out of the mist into the mirk
    The glimmering combers roll.
Almost these mindless waters work
    As though they had a soul—
Almost as though they leagued to whelm
    Our flag beneath their green:
Then welcome Fate's discourtesy
    Whereby it shall be seen, etc.

Be well assured, though wave and wind
    Have mightier blows in store,
That we who keep the watch assigned
    Must stand to it the more;

And as our streaming bows rebuke
   Each billow's baulked career,
Sing, welcome Fate's discourtesy
   Whereby it is made clear, etc.

No matter though our decks be swept
   And mast and timber crack—
We can make good all loss except
   The loss of turning back.
So, 'twixt these Devils and our deep
   Let courteous trumpets sound,
To welcome Fate's discourtesy
   Whereby it will be found, etc.

Be well assured, though in our power
   Is nothing left to give
But chance and place to meet the hour,
   And leave to strive to live,
Till these dissolve our Order holds,
   Our Service binds us here.
Then welcome Fate's discourtesy
   Whereby it is made clear
     How in all time of our distress,
     As in our triumph too,
     The game is more than the player of the game,
     And the ship is more than the crew!

THE LAST CHANTEY
1892

'And there was no more sea.'

Thus said the Lord in the Vault above the Cherubim,
  Calling to the Angels and the Souls in their degree:
   'Lo! Earth has passed away
   On the smoke of Judgment Day.
  That Our word may be established shall We gather up
    the sea?'

Loud sang the souls of the jolly, jolly mariners:
  'Plague upon the hurricane that made us furl and flee!
   But the war is done between us,
   In the deep the Lord hath seen us—
  Our bones we'll leave the barracout', and God may sink
    the sea!'

Then said the soul of Judas that betrayèd Him:
  'Lord, hast Thou forgotten Thy covenant with me?
   How once a year I go
   To cool me on the floe?
  And Ye take my day of mercy if Ye take away the sea.'

Then said the soul of the Angel of the Off-shore Wind:
  (He that bits the thunder when the bull-mouthed
    breakers flee):
   'I have watch and ward to keep
   O'er Thy wonders on the deep,
  And Ye take mine honour from me if Ye take away the
    sea!'

Loud sang the souls of the jolly, jolly mariners:
  'Nay, but we were angry, and a hasty folk are we.

If we worked the ship together
Till she foundered in foul weather,
Are we babes that we should clamour for a vengeance
on the sea?'

Then said the souls of the slaves that men threw overboard:
'Kennelled in the picaroon a weary band were we;
But Thy arm was strong to save,
And it touched us on the wave,
And we drowsed the long tides idle till Thy Trumpets
tore the sea.'

Then cried the soul of the stout Apostle Paul to God:
'Once we frapped a ship, and she laboured woundily.
There were fourteen score of these,
And they blessed Thee on their knees,
When they learned Thy Grace and Glory under Malta
by the sea!'

Loud sang the souls of the jolly, jolly mariners,
Plucking at their harps, and they plucked unhandily:
'Our thumbs are rough and tarred,
And the tune is something hard—
May we lift a Deepsea Chantey such as seamen use at
sea?'

Then said the souls of the gentlemen-adventurers—
Fettered wrist to bar all for red iniquity:
'Ho, we revel in our chains
O'er the sorrow that was Spain's!
Heave or sink it, leave or drink it, we were masters of
the sea!'

Up spake the soul of a grey Gothavn 'speckshioner—
(He that led the flenching in the fleets of fair Dundee)

'Oh, the ice-blink white and near,
And the bowhead breaching clear!
Will Ye whelm them all for wantonness that wallow in
    the sea?'

Loud sang the souls of the jolly, jolly mariners,
    Crying: 'Under Heaven, here is neither lead nor lee!
        Must we sing for evermore
        On the windless, glassy floor?
    Take back your golden fiddles and we'll beat to open
        sea!'

Then stooped the Lord, and He called the good sea up to
    Him,
    And 'stablishèd its borders unto all eternity,
        That such as have no pleasure
        For to praise the Lord by measure,
    They may enter into galleons and serve Him on the sea.

Sun, Wind, and Cloud shall fail not from the face of it,
    Stinging, ringing spindrift, nor the fulmar flying free ;
        And the ships shall go abroad
        To the Glory of the Lord
    Who heard the silly sailor-folk and gave them back their
        sea!

THE LONG TRAIL

There's a whisper down the field where the year has
    shot her yield,
    And the ricks stand grey to the sun,
Singing: 'Over then, come over, for the bee has quit the
    clover,
    'And your English summer's done.'

You have heard the beat of the off-shore wind,
And the thresh of the deep-sea rain;
You have heard the song—how long? how long?
Pull out on the trail again!
Ha' done with the Tents of Shem, dear lass,
We've seen the seasons through,
And it's time to turn on the old trail, our own trail,
the out trail,
Pull out, pull out, on the Long Trail—the trail that is
always new!

It's North you may run to the rime-ringed sun
Or South to the blind Horn's hate;
Or East all the way into Mississippi Bay,
Or West to the Golden Gate—
Where the blindest bluffs hold good, dear lass,
And the wildest tales are true,
And the men bulk big on the old trail, our own trail,
the out trail,
And life runs large on the Long Trail—the trail
that is always new.

The days are sick and cold, and the skies are grey and old
And the twice-breathed airs blow damp;
And I'd sell my tired soul for the bucking beam-sea roll
Of a black Bilbao tramp,
With her load-line over her hatch, dear lass,
And a drunken Dago crew,
And her nose held down on the old trail, our own
trail, the out trail
From Cadiz south on the Long Trail—the trail that
is always new.

There be triple ways to take, of the eagle or the snake,
Or the way of a man with a maid;

But the sweetest way to me is a ship's upon the sea
  In the heel of the North-East Trade.
      Can you hear the crash on her bows, dear lass,
      And the drum of the racing screw,
      As she ships it green on the old trail, our own trail,
        the out trail,
      As she lifts and 'scends on the Long Trail—the trail
        that is always new?

See the shaking funnels roar, with the Peter at the fore,
  And the fenders grind and heave,
And the derricks clack and grate, as the tackle hooks the
    crate,
  And the fall-rope whines through the sheave;
      It's 'Gang-plank up and in,' dear lass,
      It's 'Hawsers warp her through!'
      And it's 'All clear aft' on the old trail, our own
        trail, the out trail,
      We're backing down on the Long Trail—the trail
        that is always new.

O the mutter overside, when the port-fog holds us tied,
  And the sirens hoot their dread,
When foot by foot we creep o'er the hueless, viewless deep
  To the sob of the questing lead!
      It's down by the Lower Hope, dear lass,
      With the Gunfleet Sands in view,
      Till the Mouse swings green on the old trail, our
        own trail, the out trail,
      And the Gull Light lifts on the Long Trail—the
        trail that is always new.

O the blazing tropic night, when the wake's a welt of light
  That holds the hot sky tame,
And the steady fore-foot snores through the planet-
    powdered floors

Where the scared whale flukes in flame!
>Her plates are flaked by the sun, dear lass,
>And her ropes are taut with the dew,
>For we're booming down on the old trail, our own
>trail, the out trail,
>We're sagging south on the Long Trail—the trail
>that is always new.

Then home, get her home, where the drunken rollers comb,
>And the shouting seas drive by,
And the engines stamp and ring, and the wet bows reel
>and swing,
>And the Southern Cross rides high!
>>Yes, the old lost stars wheel back, dear lass,
>>That blaze in the velvet blue.
>>They're all old friends on the old trail, our own
>>trail, the out trail,
>>They're God's own guides on the Long Trail—the
>>trail that is always new.

Fly forward, O my heart, from the Foreland to the Start—
>We're steaming all too slow,
And it's twenty thousand mile to our little lazy isle
>Where the trumpet-orchids blow!
>>You have heard the call of the off-shore wind
>>And the voice of the deep-sea rain;
>>You have heard the song—how long?—how long?
>>Pull out on the trail again!

The Lord knows what we may find, dear lass,
And The Deuce knows what we may do—
But we're back once more on the old trail, our own trail,
>the out trail,
We're down, hull-down, on the Long Trail—the trail that
>is always new!

85

AVE IMPERATRIX!

(Written on the occasion of the attempt to assassinate Queen Victoria in March 1882)

From every quarter of your land
   They give God thanks who turned away
Death and the needy madman's hand,
   Death-fraught, which menaced you that day.

One school of many made to make
   Men who shall hold it dearest right
To battle for their ruler's sake,
   And stake their being in the fight,

Sends greeting humble and sincere—
   Though verse be rude and poor and mean—
To you, the greatest as most dear—
   Victoria, by God's grace Our Queen!

Such greeting as should come from those
   Whose fathers faced the Sepoy hordes,
Or served you in the Russian snows,
   And, dying, left their sons their swords.

And some of us have fought for you
   Already in the Afghan pass—
Or where the scarce-seen smoke-puffs flew
   From Boer marksmen in the grass;

And all are bred to do your will
   By land and sea—wherever flies
The Flag, to fight and follow still,
   And work your Empire's destinies.

Once more we greet you, though unseen
    Our greeting be, and coming slow.
Trust us, if need arise, O Queen,
    We shall not tarry with the blow!

A SONG OF THE ENGLISH
1893

Fair is our lot—O goodly is our heritage!
    (Humble ye, my people, and be fearful in your
        mirth!)
  For the Lord our God Most High
  He hath made the deep as dry,
He hath smote for us a pathway to the ends of all the Earth!

Yea, though we sinned, and our rulers went from righteous-
        ness—
Deep in all dishonour though we stained our garments' hem,
  Oh, be ye not dismayed,
  Though we stumbled and we strayed,
We were led by evil counsellors—the Lord shall deal with
        them!

Hold ye the Faith—the Faith our Fathers sealèd us;
Whoring not with visions—overwise and overstale.
  Except ye pay the Lord
  Single heart and single sword,
Of your children in their bondage He shall ask them treble-
        tale!

Keep ye the Law—be swift in all obedience—
Clear the land of evil, drive the road and bridge the ford.

Make ye sure to each his own
That he reap where he hath sown ;
By the peace among Our peoples let men know we serve the
Lord!

. . . .

Hear now a song—a song of broken interludes—
A song of little cunning; of a singer nothing worth.
Through the naked words and mean
May ye see the truth between,
As the singer knew and touched it in the ends of all the
Earth!

The Coastwise Lights

Our brows are bound with spindrift and the weed is on
  our knees;
Our loins are battered 'neath us by the swinging smoking
  seas.
From reef and rock and skerry—over headland, ness, and
  voe—
The Coastwise Lights of England watch the ships of Eng-
  land go!

Through the endless summer evenings, on the lineless,
  level floors;
Through the yelling Channel tempest when the siren hoots
  and roars—
By day the dipping house-flag and by night the rocket's
  trail—
As the sheep that graze behind us so we know them where
  they hail.

We bridge across the dark, and bid the helmsman have a
  care,
The flash that, wheeling inland, wakes his sleeping wife to
  prayer.

From our vexed eyries, head to gale, we bind in burning
  chains
The lover from the sea-rim drawn—his love in English
  lanes.

We greet the clippers wing-and-wing that race the Southern
  wool;
We warn the crawling cargo-tanks of Bremen, Leith, and
  Hull;
To each and all our equal lamp at peril of the sea—
The white wall-sided warships or the whalers of Dundee!

Come up, come in from Eastward, from the guardports of
  the Morn!
Beat up, beat in from Southerly, O gipsies of the Horn!
Swift shuttles of an Empire's loom that weave us main to
  main,
The Coastwise Lights of England give you welcome back
  again!

Go, get you gone up-Channel with the sea-crust on your
  plates;
Go, get you into London with the burden of your freights!
Haste, for they talk of Empire there, and say, if any
  seek,
The Lights of England sent you and by silence shall ye
  speak!

The Song of the Dead

*Hear now the Song of the Dead—in the North by the torn
  berg-edges—*
*They that look still to the Pole, asleep by their hide-stripped
  sledges.*

Song of the Dead in the South—in the sun by their skeleton
*   horses,*
Where the warrigal whimpers and bays through the dust of
*   the sere river-courses.*

Song of the Dead in the East—in the heat-rotted jungle-
*   hollows,*
Where the dog-ape barks in the kloof—in the brake of the
*   buffalo-wallows.*

Song of the Dead in the West—in the Barrens, the pass that
*   betrayed them,*
Where the wolverine tumbles their packs from the camp and
*   the grave-mound they made them;*
*   Hear now the Song of the Dead!*

I

We were dreamers, dreaming greatly, in the man-stifled
    town;
We yearned beyond the sky-line where the strange roads
    go down.
Came the Whisper, came the Vision, came the Power with
    the Need,
Till the Soul that is not man's soul was lent us to lead.
As the deer breaks—as the steer breaks—from the herd
    where they graze,
In the faith of little children we went on our ways.
Then the wood failed—then the food failed—then the last
    water dried—
In the faith of little children we lay down and died.
On the sand-drift—on the veldt-side—in the fern-scrub we
    lay,
That our sons might follow after by the bones on the
    way.
Follow after—follow after! We have watered the root,
And the bud has come to blossom that ripens for fruit!

90

Follow after—we are waiting, by the trails that we lost,
For the sounds of many footsteps, for the tread of a
     host.
Follow after—follow after—for the harvest is sown:
By the bones about the wayside ye shall come to your own!

> When Drake went down to the Horn
>   And England was crowned thereby,
> 'Twixt seas unsailed and shores unhailed
>   Our Lodge—our Lodge was born
>   (And England was crowned thereby!)

> Which never shall close again
>   By day nor yet by night,
> While man shall take his life to stake
>   At risk of shoal or main
>   (By day nor yet by night)

> But standeth even so
>   As now we witness here,
> While men depart, of joyful heart,
>   Adventure for to know
>   (As now bear witness here!)

II

We have fed our sea for a thousand years
     And she calls us, still unfed,
Though there's never a wave of all her waves
     But marks our English dead:
We have strawed our best to the weed's unrest,
     To the shark and the sheering gull.
If blood be the price of admiralty,
     Lord God, we ha' paid in full!

There's never a flood goes shoreward now
  But lifts a keel we manned;
There's never an ebb goes seaward now
  But drops our dead on the sand—
But slinks our dead on the sands forlore,
  From the Ducies to the Swin.
If blood be the price of admiralty,
If blood be the price of admiralty,
  Lord God, we ha' paid it in!

We must feed our sea for a thousand years,
  For that is our doom and pride,
As it was when they sailed with the *Golden Hind*,
  Or the wreck that struck last tide—
Or the wreck that lies on the spouting reef
  Where the ghastly blue-lights flare.
If blood be the price of admiralty,
If blood be the price of admiralty,
If blood be the price of admiralty,
  Lord God, we ha' bought it fair!

The Deep-Sea Cables

The wrecks dissolve above us; their dust drops down
    from afar—
Down to the dark, to the utter dark, where the blind white
    sea-snakes are.
There is no sound, no echo of sound, in the deserts of the
    deep,
Or the great grey level plains of ooze where the shell-
    burred cables creep.

Here in the womb of the world—here on the tie-ribs of
    earth
  Words, and the words of men, flicker and flutter and
    beat—

92

Warning, sorrow, and gain, salutation and mirth—
　　For a Power troubles the Still that has neither voice nor
　　　feet.

They have wakened the timeless Things; they have killed
　　their father Time;
　　Joining hands in the gloom, a league from the last of the
　　　sun.
Hush! Men talk to-day o'er the waste of the ultimate
　　slime,
　　And a new Word runs between: whispering, 'Let us be
　　　one!'

The Song of the Sons

One from the ends of the earth—gifts at an open
　　door—
Treason has much, but we, Mother, thy sons have more!
From the whine of a dying man, from the snarl of a wolf-
　　pack freed,
Turn, and the world is thine. Mother, be proud of thy
　　seed!
Count, are we feeble or few? Hear, is our speech so rude?
Look, are we poor in the land? Judge, are we men of The
　　Blood?

Those that have stayed at thy knees, Mother, go call them
　　in—
We that were bred overseas wait and would speak with our
　　kin.
Not in the dark do we fight—haggle and flout and gibe;
Selling our love for a price, loaning our hearts for a
　　bribe.
Gifts have we only to-day—Love without promise or fee—
Hear, for thy children speak, from the uttermost parts of
　　the sea!

The Song of the Cities

BOMBAY

Royal and Dower-royal, I the Queen
  Fronting thy richest sea with richer hands—
A thousand mills roar through me where I glean
  All races from all lands.

CALCUTTA

Me the Sea-captain loved, the River built,
  Wealth sought and Kings adventured life to hold.
Hail, England! I am Asia—Power on silt,
  Death in my hands, but Gold!

MADRAS

Clive kissed me on the mouth and eyes and brow,
  Wonderful kisses, so that I became
Crowned above Queens—a withered beldame now,
  Brooding on ancient fame.

RANGOON

Hail, Mother! Do they call me rich in trade?
  Little care I, but hear the shorn priest drone,
And watch my silk-clad lovers, man by maid,
  Laugh 'neath my Shwe Dagon.

SINGAPORE

Hail, Mother! East and West must seek my aid
  Ere the spent hull may dare the ports afar.
The second doorway of the wide world's trade
  Is mine to loose or bar.

HONG-KONG

Hail, Mother! Hold me fast; my Praya sleeps
   Under innumerable keels to-day.
Yet guard (and landward), or to-morrow sweeps
   Thy warships down the bay!

HALIFAX

Into the mist my guardian prows put forth,
   Behind the mist my virgin ramparts lie,
The Warden of the Honour of the North,
   Sleepless and veiled am I!

QUEBEC AND MONTREAL

Peace is our portion. Yet a whisper rose,
   Foolish and causeless, half in jest, half hate.
Now wake we and remember mighty blows,
   And, fearing no man, wait!

VICTORIA

From East to West the circling word has passed,
   Till West is East beside our land-locked blue;
From East to West the tested chain holds fast,
   The well-forged link rings true!

CAPETOWN

Hail! Snatched and bartered oft from hand to
   hand,
   I dream my dream, by rock and heath and pine,
Of Empire to the northward. Ay, one land
   From Lion's Head to Line!

MELBOURNE

Greeting! Nor fear nor favour won us place,
  Got between greed of gold and dread of drouth,
Loud-voiced and reckless as the wild tide-race
  That whips our harbour-mouth!

SYDNEY

Greeting! My birth-stain have I turned to good;
  Forcing strong wills perverse to steadfastness:
The first flush of the tropics in my blood,
  And at my feet Success!

BRISBANE

The northern stock beneath the southern skies—
  I build a Nation for an Empire's need,
Suffer a little, and my land shall rise,
  Queen over lands indeed!

HOBART

Man's love first found me; man's hate made me Hell;
  For my babes' sake I cleansed those infamies.
Earnest for leave to live and labour well,
  God flung me peace and ease.

AUCKLAND

Last, loneliest, loveliest, exquisite, apart—
  On us, on us the unswerving season smiles,
Who wonder 'mid our fern why men depart
  To seek the Happy Isles!

Truly ye come of The Blood, slower to bless than to ban,
Little used to lie down at the bidding of any man—
Flesh of the flesh that I bred, bone of the bone that I bare;
Stark as your sons shall be—stern as your fathers were.
Deeper than speech our love, stronger than life our tether,
But we do not fall on the neck nor kiss when we come
    together.
My arm is nothing weak, my strength is not gone by;
Sons, I have borne many sons, but my dugs are not dry.
Look, I have made ye a place and opened wide the doors,
That ye may talk together, your Barons and Councillors—
Wards of the Outer March, Lords of the Lower Seas,
Ay, talk to your grey mother that bore you on her knees!—
That ye may talk together, brother to brother's face—
Thus for the good of your peoples—thus for the Pride of
    the Race.
Also, we will make promise. So long as The Blood endures,
I shall know that your good is mine: ye shall feel that my
    strength is yours:
In the day of Armageddon, at the last great fight of all,
That Our House stand together and the pillars do not
    fall.
Draw now the threefold knot firm on the ninefold bands,
And the Law that ye make shall be law after the rule of
    your lands.
This for the waxen Heath, and that for the Wattle-bloom,
This for the Maple-Leaf, and that for the Southern Broom.
The Law that ye make shall be law and I do not press my
    will,
Because ye are Sons of The Blood and call me Mother still.
Now must ye speak to your kinsmen and they must speak
    to you,
After the use of the English, in straight-flung words and
    few.

Go to your work and be strong, halting not in your ways,
Baulking the end half-won for an instant dole of praise.
Stand to your work and be wise—certain of sword and pen,
Who are neither children nor Gods, but men in a world of
      men!

THE GIPSY TRAIL

The white moth to the closing bine,
    The bee to the opened clover,
And the gipsy blood to the gipsy blood
    Ever the wide world over.

Ever the wide world over, lass,
    Ever the trail held true,
Over the world and under the world,
    And back at the last to you.

Out of the dark of the gorgio camp,
    Out of the grime and the gray
(Morning waits at the end of the world),
    Gipsy, come away!

The wild boar to the sun-dried swamp,
    The red crane to her reed,
And the Romany lass to the Romany lad
    By the tie of a roving breed.

The pied snake to the rifted rock,
    The buck to the stony plain,
And the Romany lass to the Romany lad,
    And both to the road again.

Both to the road again, again!
    Out on a clean sea-track—
Follow the cross of the gipsy trail
    Over the world and back!

Follow the Romany patteran
　　North where the blue bergs sail,
And the bows are gray with the frozen spray,
　　And the masts are shod with mail.

Follow the Romany patteran
　　Sheer to the Austral Light,
Where the besom of God is the wild South wind,
　　Sweeping the sea-floors white.

Follow the Romany patteran
　　West to the sinking sun,
Till the junk-sails lift through the houseless drift,
　　And the east and the west are one.

Follow the Romany patteran
　　East where the silence broods
By a purple wave on an opal beach
　　In the hush of the Mahim woods.

'The wild hawk to the wind-swept sky,
　　The deer to the wholesome wold,
And the heart of a man to the heart of a maid,
　　As it was in the days of old.'

The heart of a man to the heart of a maid—
　　Light of my tents, be fleet.
Morning waits at the end of the world,
　　And the world is all at our feet!

OUR LADY OF THE SNOWS

1897

(Canadian Preferential Tariff, 1897)

A Nation spoke to a Nation,
  A Queen sent word to a Throne:
'Daughter am I in my mother's house,
  But mistress in my own.
The gates are mine to open,
  As the gates are mine to close,
And I set my house in order,'
  Said our Lady of the Snows.

'Neither with laughter nor weeping,
  Fear or the child's amaze—
Soberly under the White Man's law
  My white men go their ways.
Not for the Gentiles' clamour—
  Insult or threat of blows—
Bow we the knee to Baal,'
  Said our Lady of the Snows.

'My speech is clean and single,
  I talk of common things—
Words of the wharf and the market-place
  And the ware the merchant brings:
Favour to those I favour,
  But a stumbling-block to my foes.
Many there be that hate us,'
  Said our Lady of the Snows.

'I called my chiefs to council
  In the din of a troubled year;
For the sake of a sign ye would not see,
  And a word ye would not hear.

This is our message and answer;
   This is the path we chose:
For we be also a people,'
   Said our Lady of the Snows.

'Carry the word to my sisters—
   To the Queens of the East and the South.
I have proven faith in the Heritage
   By more than the word of the mouth.
They that are wise may follow
   Ere the world's war-trumpet blows,
But I—I am first in the battle,'
   Said our Lady of the Snows.

A Nation spoke to a Nation,
   A Throne sent word to a Throne :
'Daughter am I in my mother's house,
   But mistress in my own.
The gates are mine to open,
   As the gates are mine to close,
And I abide by my Mother's House,'
   Said our Lady of the Snows.

THE IRISH GUARDS
1918

We're not so old in the Army List,
    But we're not so young at our trade,
For we had the honour at Fontenoy
    Of meeting the Guards' Brigade.
'Twas Lally, Dillon, Bulkeley, Clare,
    And Lee that led us then,
And after a hundred and seventy years
    We're fighting for France again!
      Old Days! The wild geese are flighting,
        Head to the storm as they faced it before!
      For where there are Irish there's bound to be fighting,
        And when there's no fighting, it's Ireland no more!
                Ireland no more!

The fashion's all for khaki now,
    But once through France we went
Full-dressed in scarlet Army cloth
    The English—left at Ghent.
They're fighting on our side to-day
    But, before they changed their clothes,
The half of Europe knew our fame,
    As all of Ireland knows!
      Old Days! The wild geese are flying,
        Head to the storm as they faced it before!
      For where there are Irish there's memory undying,
        And when we forget, it is Ireland no more!
                Ireland no more!

From Barry Wood to Gouzeaucourt,
    From Boyne to Pilkem Ridge
The ancient days come back no more
    Than water under the bridge.

But the bridge it stands and the water runs
    As red as yesterday,
And the Irish move to the sound of the guns
    Like salmon to the sea.
        Old Days! The wild geese are ranging,
          Head to the storm as they faced it before!
        For where there are Irish their hearts are unchanging,
          And when they are changed, it is Ireland no more!
                        Ireland no more!

We're not so old in the Army List,
    But we're not so new in the ring,
For we carried our packs with Marshal Saxe
    When Louis was our King.
But Douglas Haig's our Marshal now
    And we're King George's men,
And after one hundred and seventy years
    We're fighting for France again!
        Ah, France! And did we stand by you,
          When life was made splendid with gifts and rewards?
        Ah, France! And will we deny you
          In the hour of your agony, Mother of Swords?
        Old Days! The wild geese are flighting,
          Head to the storm as they faced it before!
        For where there are Irish there's loving and fighting,
          And when we stop either, it's Ireland no more!
                        Ireland no more!

THE SETTLER

1903

(*South African War ended, May* 1902)

Here, where my fresh-turned furrows run,
    And the deep soil glistens red,
I will repair the wrong that was done
    To the living and the dead.

Here, where the senseless bullet fell,
    And the barren shrapnel burst,
I will plant a tree, I will dig a well,
    Against the heat and the thirst.

Here, in a large and a sunlit land,
    Where no wrong bites to the bone,
I will lay my hand in my neighbour's hand.
    And together we will atone
For the set folly and the red breach
    And the black waste of it all;
Giving and taking counsel each
    Over the cattle-kraal.

Here will we join against our foes—
    The hailstroke and the storm,
And the red and rustling cloud that blows
    The locust's mile-deep swarm.
Frost and murrain and flood let loose
    Shall launch us side by side
In the holy wars that have no truce
    'Twixt seed and harvest-tide.

Earth, where we rode to slay or be slain,
    Our love shall redeem unto life.
We will gather and lead to her lips again
    The waters of ancient strife,
From the far and the fiercely guarded streams
    And the pools where we lay in wait,
Till the corn cover our evil dreams
    And the young corn our hate.

And when we bring old fights to mind,
    We will not remember the sin—
If there be blood on his head of my kind,
    Or blood on my head of his kin—

For the ungrazed upland, the untilled lea
   Cry, and the fields forlorn:
'The dead must bury their dead, but ye—
   Ye serve an host unborn.'

Bless then, Our God, the new-yoked plough
   And the good beasts that draw,
And the bread we eat in the sweat of our brow
   According to Thy Law.
After us cometh a multitude—
   Prosper the work of our hands,
That we may feed with our land's food
   The folk of all our lands!

Here, in the waves and the troughs of the plains
   Where the healing stillness lies,
And the vast, benignant sky restrains
   And the long days make wise—
Bless to our use the rain and the sun
   And the blind seed in its bed,
That we may repair the wrong that was done
   To the living and the dead!

SUSSEX

1902

God gave all men all earth to love,
   But, since our hearts are small,
Ordained for each one spot should prove
   Belovèd over all;
That, as He watched Creation's birth,
   So we, in godlike mood,
May of our love create our earth
   And see that it is good.

105

So one shall Baltic pines content,
 As one some Surrey glade,
Or one the palm-grove's droned lament
 Before Levuka's Trade.
Each to his choice, and I rejoice
 The lot has fallen to me
In a fair ground—in a fair ground—
 Yea, Sussex by the sea!

No tender-hearted garden crowns,
 No bosomed woods adorn
Our blunt, bow-headed, whale-backed Downs,
 But gnarled and writhen thorn—
Bare slopes where chasing shadows skim,
 And, through the gaps revealed,
Belt upon belt, the wooded, dim,
 Blue goodness of the Weald.

Clean of officious fence or hedge,
 Half-wild and wholly tame,
The wise turf cloaks the white cliff-edge
 As when the Romans came.
What sign of those that fought and died
 At shift of sword and sword?
The barrow and the camp abide,
 The sunlight and the sward.

Here leaps ashore the full Sou'west
 All heavy-winged with brine,
Here lies above the folded crest
 The Channel's leaden line;
And here the sea-fogs lap and cling,
 And here, each warning each,
The sheep-bells and the ship-bells ring
 Along the hidden beach.

We have no waters to delight
　　Our broad and brookless vales—
Only the dewpond on the height
　　Unfed, that never fails—
Whereby no tattered herbage tells
　　Which way the season flies—
Only our close-bit thyme that smells
　　Like dawn in Paradise.

Here through the strong and shadeless days
　　The tinkling silence thrills;
Or little, lost, Down churches praise
　　The Lord who made the hills:
But here the Old Gods guard their round,
　　And, in her secret heart,
The heathen kingdom Wilfrid found
　　Dreams, as she dwells, apart.

Though all the rest were all my share,
　　With equal soul I'd see
Her nine-and-thirty sisters fair,
　　Yet none more fair than she.
Choose ye your need from Thames to Tweed,
　　And I will choose instead
Such lands as lie 'twixt Rake and Rye,
　　Black Down and Beachy Head.

I will go out against the sun
　　Where the rolled scarp retires,
And the Long Man of Wilmington
　　Looks naked toward the shires;
And east till doubling Rother crawls
　　To find the fickle tide,
By dry and sea-forgotten walls,
　　Our ports of stranded pride.

I will go north about the shaws
   And the deep ghylls that breed
Huge oaks and old, the which we hold
   No more than Sussex weed;
Or south where windy Piddinghoe's
   Begilded dolphin veers,
And red beside wide-bankèd Ouse
   Lie down our Sussex steers.

So to the land our hearts we give
   Till the sure magic strike,
And Memory, Use, and Love make live
   Us and our fields alike—
That deeper than our speech and thought,
   Beyond our reason's sway,
Clay of the pit whence we were wrought
   Yearns to its fellow-clay.

God gives all men all earth to love,
   But, since man's heart is small,
Ordains for each one spot shall prove
   Belovèd over all.
Each to his choice, and I rejoice
   The lot has fallen to me
In a fair ground—in a fair ground—
   Yea, Sussex by the sea!

THE VAMPIRE
1897

A fool there was and he made his prayer
   (Even as you and I!)
To a rag and a bone and a hank of hair
(We called her the woman who did not care)
But the fool he called her his lady fair—
   (Even as you and I!)

Oh, the years we waste and the tears we waste
And the work of our head and hand
Belong to the woman who did not know
(And now we know that she never could know)
And did not understand!

A fool there was and his goods he spent
(Even as you and I!)
Honour and faith and a sure intent
(And it wasn't the least what the lady meant)
But a fool must follow his natural bent
(Even as you and I!)

Oh, the toil we lost and the spoil we lost
And the excellent things we planned
Belong to the woman who didn't know why
(And now we know that she never knew why)
And did not understand!

The fool was stripped to his foolish hide
(Even as you and I!)
Which she might have seen when she threw him aside—
(But it isn't on record the lady tried)
So some of him lived but the most of him died—
(Even as you and I!)

And it isn't the shame and it isn't the blame
That stings like a white-hot brand—
It's coming to know that she never knew why
(Seeing, at last, she could never know why)
And never could understand!

WHEN EARTH'S LAST PICTURE IS PAINTED

1892

(*L'Envoi to 'The Seven Seas'*)

When Earth's last picture is painted and the tubes are
    twisted and dried,
When the oldest colours have faded, and the youngest
    critic has died,
We shall rest, and, faith, we shall need it—lie down for an
    æon or two,
Till the Master of All Good Workmen shall put us to work
    anew.

And those that were good shall be happy: they shall sit in
    a golden chair;
They shall splash at a ten-league canvas with brushes of
    comets' hair.
They shall find real saints to draw from—Magdalene,
    Peter, and Paul;
They shall work for an age at a sitting and never be tired
    at all!

And only The Master shall praise us, and only The Master
    shall blame;
And no one shall work for money, and no one shall work
    for fame,
But each for the joy of the working, and each, in his
    separate star,
Shall draw the Thing as he sees It for the God of Things as
    They are!

THE BALLAD OF EAST AND WEST

1889

*Oh, East is East, and West is West, and never the twain
      shall meet,
Till Earth and Sky stand presently at God's great Judgment
      Seat;
But there is neither East nor West, Border, nor Breed, nor
      Birth,
When two strong men stand face to face, though they come
      from the ends of the earth!*

Kamal is out with twenty men to raise the Border-side,
And he has lifted the Colonel's mare that is the Colonel's
      pride.
He has lifted her out of the stable-door between the dawn
      and the day,
And turned the calkins upon her feet, and ridden her far
      away.
Then up and spoke the Colonel's son that led a troop of
      the Guides:
'Is there never a man of all my men can say where Kamal
      hides?'
Then up and spoke Mohammed Khan, the son of the
      Ressaldar:
'If ye know the track of the morning-mist, ye know where
      his pickets are.
 At dusk he harries the Abazai—at dawn he is into Bonair,
 But he must go by Fort Bukloh to his own place to fare.
 So if ye gallop to Fort Bukloh as fast as a bird can fly,
 By the favour of God ye may cut him off ere he win to
      the Tongue of Jagai.
 But if he be past the Tongue of Jagai, right swiftly turn
      ye then,
 For the length and the breadth of that grisly plain is sown
      with Kamal's men.

There is rock to the left, and rock to the right, and low
lean thorn between,
And ye may hear a breech-bolt snick where never a man
is seen.'
The Colonel's son has taken horse, and a raw rough dun
was he,
With the mouth of a bell and the heart of Hell and the head
of a gallows-tree.
The Colonel's son to the Fort has won, they bid him stay
to eat—
Who rides at the tail of a Border thief, he sits not long at
his meat.
He's up and away from Fort Bukloh as fast as he can
fly,
Till he was aware of his father's mare in the gut of the
Tongue of Jagai,
Till he was aware of his father's mare with Kamal upon
her back,
And when he could spy the white of her eye, he made the
pistol crack.
He has fired once, he has fired twice, but the whistling ball
went wide.
'Ye shoot like a soldier,' Kamal said. 'Show now if ye
can ride!'
It's up and over the Tongue of Jagai, as blown dust-devils
go,
The dun he fled like a stag of ten, but the mare like a
barren doe.
The dun he leaned against the bit and slugged his head
above,
But the red mare played with the snaffle-bars, as a maiden
plays with a glove.
There was rock to the left and rock to the right, and low
lean thorn between,
And thrice he heard a breech-bolt snick tho' never a man
was seen.

They have ridden the low moon out of the sky, their hoofs
      drum up the dawn,
The dun he went like a wounded bull, but the mare like a
      new-roused fawn.
The dun he fell at a water-course—in a woeful heap fell
      he,
And Kamal has turned the red mare back, and pulled the
      rider free.
He has knocked the pistol out of his hand—small room was
      there to strive,
"'Twas only by favour of mine,' quoth he, 'ye rode so
      long alive:
'There was not a rock for twenty mile, there was not a
      clump of tree,
'But covered a man of my own men with his rifle cocked
      on his knee.
'If I had raised my bridle-hand, as I have held it
      low,
'The little jackals that flee so fast were feasting all in a
      row.
'If I had bowed my head on my breast, as I have held it
      high,
'The kite that whistles above us now were gorged till she
      could not fly.'
Lightly answered the Colonel's son: 'Do good to bird and
      beast,
'But count who come for the broken meats before thou
      makest a feast.
'If there should follow a thousand swords to carry my
      bones away,
'Belike the price of a jackal's meal were more than a thief
      could pay.
'They will feed their horse on the standing crop, their
      men on the garnered grain.
'The thatch of the byres will serve their fires when all the
      cattle are slain.

113

'But if thou thinkest the price be fair,—thy brethren wait
    to sup,
'The hound is kin to the jackal-spawn,—howl, dog, and
    call them up!
'And if thou thinkest the price be high, in steer and gear
    and stack,
'Give me my father's mare again, and I'll fight my own
    way back!'
Kamal has gripped him by the hand and set him upon his
    feet.
'No talk shall be of dogs,' said he, 'when wolf and grey
    wolf meet.
'May I eat dirt if thou hast hurt of me in deed or
    breath;
'What dam of lances brought thee forth to jest at the
    dawn with Death?'
Lightly answered the Colonel's son: 'I hold by the blood
    of my clan:
'Take up the mare for my father's gift—by God, she has
    carried a man!'
The red mare ran to the Colonel's son, and nuzzled against
    his breast;
'We be two strong men,' said Kamal then, 'but she
    loveth the younger best.
'So she shall go with a lifter's dower, my turquoise-
    studded rein,
'My 'broidered saddle and saddle-cloth, and silver stir-
    rups twain.'
The Colonel's son a pistol drew, and held it muzzle-
    end,
'Ye have taken the one from a foe,' said he. 'Will ye
    take the mate from a friend?'
'A gift for a gift,' said Kamal straight; 'a limb for the
    risk of a limb.
'Thy father has sent his son to me, I'll send my son to
    him!'

With that he whistled his only son, that dropped from a
         mountain-crest—
He trod the ling like a buck in spring, and he looked like a
         lance in rest.
'Now here is thy master,' Kamal said, 'who leads a troop
         of the Guides,
'And thou must ride at his left side as shield on shoulder
         rides.
'Till Death or I cut loose the tie, at camp and board and
         bed,
'Thy life is his—thy fate it is to guard him with thy
         head.
'So, thou must eat the White Queen's meat, and all her
         foes are thine,
'And thou must harry thy father's hold for the peace of
         the Border-line.
'And thou must make a trooper tough and hack thy way
         to power—
'Belike they will raise thee to Ressaldar when I am hanged
         in Peshawur!'

They have looked each other between the eyes, and there
         they found no fault.
They have taken the Oath of the Brother-in-Blood on
         leavened bread and salt:
They have taken the Oath of the Brother-in-Blood on fire
         and fresh-cut sod,
On the hilt and the haft of the Khyber knife, and the
         Wondrous Names of God.

The Colonel's son he rides the mare and Kamal's boy the
         dun,
And two have come back to Fort Bukloh where there went
         forth but one.

And when they drew to the Quarter-Guard, full twenty
    swords flew clear—
There was not a man but carried his feud with the blood of
    the mountaineer.
'Ha' done! ha' done!' said the Colonel's son. 'Put up
    the steel at your sides!
'Last night ye had struck at a Border thief—to-night 'tis a
    man of the Guides!'

Oh, East is East, and West is West, and never the twain
    shall meet,
Till Earth and Sky stand presently at God's great Judgment
    Seat ;
But there is neither East nor West, Border, nor Breed, nor
    Birth,
When two strong men stand face to face, though they come
    from the ends of the earth!

GEHAZI

1915

Whence comest thou, Gehazi,
    So reverend to behold,
In scarlet and in ermines
    And chain of England's gold?
'From following after Naaman
    To tell him all is well,
Whereby my zeal hath made me
    A Judge in Israel.'

Well done, well done, Gehazi!
    Stretch forth thy ready hand.
Thou barely 'scaped from judgment,
    Take oath to judge the land

116

Unswayed by gift of money
  Or privy bribe, more base,
Of knowledge which is profit
  In any market-place.

Search out and probe, Gehazi,
  As thou of all canst try,
The truthful, well-weighed answer
  That tells the blacker lie—
The loud, uneasy virtue,
  The anger feigned at will,
To overbear a witness
  And make the Court keep still.

Take order now, Gehazi,
  That no man talk aside
In secret with his judges
  The while his case is tried.
Lest he should show them—reason
  To keep a matter hid,
And subtly lead the questions
  Away from what he did.

Thou mirror of uprightness,
  What ails thee at thy vows?
What means the risen whiteness
  Of the skin between thy brows?
The boils that shine and burrow,
  The sores that slough and bleed—
The leprosy of Naaman
  On thee and all thy seed?
    Stand up, stand up, Gehazi,
      Draw close thy robe and go.
    Gehazi, Judge in Israel,
      A leper white as snow!

ET DONA FERENTES

1896

In extended observation of the ways and works of man,
  From the Four-mile Radius roughly to the Plains of
    Hindustan:
I have drunk with mixed assemblies, seen the racial ruction
    rise,
And the men of half Creation damning half Creation's
    eyes.

I have watched them in their tantrums, all that pentecostal
    crew,
French, Italian, Arab, Spaniard, Dutch and Greek, and
    Russ and Jew,
Celt and savage, buff and ochre, cream and yellow, mauve
    and white,
But it never really mattered till the English grew polite;

Till the men with polished toppers, till the men in long
    frock-coats,
Till the men who do not duel, till the men who war with
    votes,
Till the breed that take their pleasures as Saint Lawrence
    took his grid,
Began to 'beg your pardon' and—the knowing croupier
    hid.

Then the bandsmen with their fiddles, and the girls that
    bring the beer,
Felt the psychological moment, left the lit Casino clear;
But the uninstructed alien, from the Teuton to the Gaul,
Was entrapped, once more, my country, by that suave,
    deceptive drawl.

.   .   .   .   .

As it was in ancient Suez or 'neath wilder, milder skies,
I 'observe with apprehension' how the racial ructions
    rise;
And with keener apprehension, if I read the times aright,
Hear the old Casino order: 'Watch your man, but be polite.

'Keep your temper. Never answer (*that* was why they
    spat and swore).
Don't hit first, but move together (there's no hurry) to the
    door.
Back to back, and facing outward while the linguist tells
    'em how—
' "*Nous sommes allong ar notre batteau, nous ne voulong pas
    un row.*" '

So the hard, pent rage ate inward, till some idiot went too
    far . . .
'Let 'em have it!' and they had it, and the same was
    merry war—
Fist, umbrella, cane, decanter, lamp and beer-mug, chair
    and boot—
Till behind the fleeing legions rose the long, hoarse yell for
    loot.

Then the oil-cloth with its numbers, like a banner fluttered
    free;
Then the grand piano cantered, on three castors, down the
    quay;
White, and breathing through their nostrils, silent, system-
    atic, swift—
They removed, effaced, abolished all that man could heave
    or lift.

Oh, my country, bless the training that from cot to castle
    runs—
The pitfall of the stranger but the bulwark of thy sons—

Measured speech and ordered action, sluggish soul and
    unperturbed,
Till we wake our Island-Devil—nowise cool for being
    curbed!

When the heir of all the ages 'has the honour to remain,'
When he will not hear an insult, though men make it ne'er
    so plain,
When his lips are schooled to meekness, when his back is
    bowed to blows—
Well the keen *aas-vogels* know it—well the waiting jackal
    knows.

Build on the flanks of Etna where the sullen smoke-puffs
    float—
Or bathe in tropic waters where the lean fin dogs the boat—
Cock the gun that is not loaded, cook the frozen dynamite—
But oh, beware my Country, when my Country grows
    polite!

THE HOLY WAR
1917

('*For here lay the excellent wisdom of him that built Mansoul, that
the walls could never be broken down nor hurt by the most
mighty adverse potentate unless the townsmen gave consent
thereto.*'—BUNYAN'S *Holy War*.)

A tinker out of Bedford,
    A vagrant oft in quod,
A private under Fairfax,
    A minister of God—
Two hundred years and thirty
    Ere Armageddon came
His single hand portrayed it,
    And Bunyan was his name

120

He mapped for those who follow,
   The world in which we are—
'This famous town of Mansoul'
   That takes the Holy War.
Her true and traitor people,
   The Gates along her wall,
From Eye Gate unto Feel Gate,
   John Bunyan showed them all.

All enemy divisions,
   Recruits of every class,
And highly screened positions
   For flame or poison-gas;
The craft that we call modern,
   The crimes that we call new,
John Bunyan had 'em typed and filed
   In Sixteen Eighty-two.

Likewise the Lords of Looseness
   That hamper faith and works,
The Perseverance-Doubters,
   And Present-Comfort shirks,
With brittle intellectuals
   Who crack beneath a strain—
John Bunyan met that helpful set
   In Charles the Second's reign

Emmanuel's vanguard dying
   For right and not for rights,
My Lord Apollyon lying
   To the State-kept Stockholmites,
The Pope, the swithering Neutrals,
   The Kaiser and his Gott—
Their rôles, their goals, their naked souls—
   He knew and drew the lot.

Now he hath left his quarters,
    In Bunhill Fields to lie,
The wisdom that he taught us
    Is proven prophecy—
One watchword through our Armies,
    One answer from our Lands:—
'No dealings with Diabolus
    As long as Mansoul stands!'

A pedlar from a hovel,
    The lowest of the low—
The Father of the Novel,
    Salvation's first Defoe—
Eight blinded generations
    Ere Armageddon came,
He showed us how to meet it,
    And Bunyan was his name!

FRANCE

1913

Broke to every known mischance, lifted over all
  By the light sane joy of life, the buckler of the Gaul;
Furious in luxury, merciless in toil,
Terrible with strength that draws from her tireless soil;
Strictest judge of her own worth, gentlest of man's mind,
First to follow Truth and last to leave old Truths behind—
France, beloved of every soul that loves its fellow-kind!

Ere our birth (rememberest thou?) side by side we lay
Fretting in the womb of Rome to begin our fray.
Ere men knew our tongues apart, our one task was
    known—
Each to mould the other's fate as he wrought his own.

To this end we stirred mankind till all Earth was ours,
Till our world-end strifes begat wayside Thrones and
　　　Powers—
Puppets that we made or broke to bar the other's path—
Necessary, outpost-folk, hirelings of our wrath.
To this end we stormed the seas, tack for tack, and burst
Through the doorways of new worlds, doubtful which was
　　　first,
Hand on hilt (rememberest thou?) ready for the blow—
Sure, whatever else we met, we should meet our foe.
Spurred or balked at every stride by the other's strength,
So we rode the ages down and every ocean's length!

Where did you refrain from us or we refrain from you?
Ask the wave that has not watched war between us two!
Others held us for a while, but with weaker charms,
These we quitted at the call for each other's arms.

Eager toward the known delight, equally we strove—
Each the other's mystery, terror, need, and love.
To each other's open court with our proofs we came.
Where could we find honour else, or men to test our claim?
From each other's throat we wrenched—valour's last
　　　reward—
That extorted word of praise gasped 'twixt lunge and
　　　guard.
In each other's cup we poured mingled blood and tears,
Brutal joys, unmeasured hopes, intolerable fears—
All that soiled or salted life for a thousand years.
Proved beyond the need of proof, matched in every clime,
O Companion, we have lived greatly through all time!

Yoked in knowledge and remorse, now we come to rest,
Laughing at old villainies that Time has turned to jest;
Pardoning old necessities no pardon can efface—
That undying sin we shared in Rouen market-place.

Now we watch the new years shape, wondering if they hold
Fiercer lightnings in their heart than we launched of old.
Now we hear new voices rise, question, boast or gird,
As we raged (rememberest thou?) when our crowds were
    stirred.
Now we count new keels afloat, and new hosts on land,
Massed like ours (rememberest thou?) when our strokes
    were planned.
We were schooled for dear life's sake, to know each other's
    blade.
What can Blood and Iron make more than we have made?
We have learned by keenest use to know each other's mind.
What shall Blood and Iron loose that we cannot bind?
We who swept each other's coast, sacked each other's
    home,
Since the sword of Brennus clashed on the scales at Rome,
Listen, count and close again, wheeling girth to girth,
In the linked and steadfast guard set for peace on earth!

Broke to every known mischance, lifted over all
By the light sane joy of life, the buckler of the Gaul;
Furious in luxury, merciless in toil,
Terrible with strength renewed from a tireless soil;
Strictest judge of her own worth, gentlest of man's mind,
First to face the Truth and last to leave old Truths behind—
France, beloved of every soul that loves or serves its kind!

THE BELL BUOY

1896

They christened my brother of old—
    And a saintly name he bears—
They gave him his place to hold
    At the head of the belfry-stairs,

On the horns of death I ride.
  A ship-length overside,
Between the course and the sand
    Fretted and bound I bide
        Peril whereof I cry.
Would I change with my brother a league inland?
(*Shoal! 'Ware shoal!*) Not I!

MESOPOTAMIA

1917

They shall not return to us, the resolute, the young,
  The eager and whole-hearted whom we gave:
But the men who left them thriftily to die in their own
      dung,
  Shall they come with years and honour to the grave?

They shall not return to us, the strong men coldly slain
  In sight of help denied from day to day:
But the men who edged their agonies and chid them in
      their pain,
  Are they too strong and wise to put away?

Our dead shall not return to us while Day and Night
      divide—
  Never while the bars of sunset hold.
But the idle-minded overlings who quibbled while they
      died,
  Shall they thrust for high employments as of old?

Shall we only threaten and be angry for an hour?
  When the storm is ended shall we find
How softly but how swiftly they have sidled back to power
  By the favour and contrivance of their kind?

127

Even while they soothe us, while they promise large
      amends,
    Even while they make a show of fear,
Do they call upon their debtors, and take counsel with
      their friends,
    To confirm and re-establish each career?

Their lives cannot repay us—their death could not undo—
    The shame that they have laid upon our race.
But the slothfulness that wasted and the arrogance that
      slew,
    Shall we leave it unabated in its place?

THE ISLANDERS
1902

*No doubt but ye are the People—your throne is above
    the King's.*
Whoso speaks in your presence must say acceptable things:
Bowing the head in worship, bending the knee in fear—
*Bringing the word well smoothen—such as a King should
    hear:*

Fenced by your careful fathers, ringed by your leaden seas,
Long did ye wake in quiet and long lie down at ease;
Till ye said of Strife, 'What is it?' of the Sword, 'It is
    far from our ken';
Till ye made a sport of your shrunken hosts and a toy of
    your armèd men.
Ye stopped your ears to the warning—ye would neither
    look nor heed—
Ye set your leisure before their toil and your lusts above
    their need.

128

Because of your witless learning and your beasts of warren
and chase,
Ye grudged your sons to their service and your fields for
their camping-place.
Ye forced them glean in the highways the straw for the
bricks they brought;
Ye forced them follow in byways the craft that ye never
taught.
Ye hampered and hindered and crippled; ye thrust out of
sight and away
Those that would serve you for honour and those that
served you for pay.
Then were the judgments loosened; then was your shame
revealed,
At the hands of a little people, few but apt in the field.
Yet ye were saved by a remnant (and your land's long-
suffering star),
When your strong men cheered in their millions while your
striplings went to the war.
Sons of the sheltered city—unmade, unhandled, unmeet—
Ye pushed them raw to the battle as ye picked them raw
from the street.
And what did ye look they should compass? Warcraft
learned in a breath,
Knowledge unto occasion at the first far view of Death?
So? And ye train your horses and the dogs ye feed and prize?
How are the beasts more worthy than the souls, your
sacrifice?
But ye said, 'Their valour shall show them'; but ye said,
'The end is close.'
And ye sent them comfits and pictures to help them harry
your foes:
And ye vaunted your fathomless power, and ye flaunted
your iron pride,
Ere—ye fawned on the Younger Nations for the men who
could shoot and ride!

Then ye returned to your trinkets; then ye contented your
    souls
With the flannelled fools at the wicket or the muddied oafs
    at the goals.
Given to strong delusion, wholly believing a lie,
Ye saw that the land lay fenceless, and ye let the months
    go by
Waiting some easy wonder, hoping some saving sign—
Idle—openly idle—in the lee of the forespent Line.
Idle—except for your boasting—and what is your boast-
    ing worth
If ye grudge a year of service to the lordliest life on
    earth?
Ancient, effortless, ordered, cycle on cycle set,
Life so long untroubled, that ye who inherit forget
It was not made with the mountains, it is not one with the
    deep.
Men, not gods, devised it. Men, not gods, must keep.
Men, not children, servants, or kinsfolk called from afar,
But each man born in the Island broke to the matter of
    war.
Soberly and by custom taken and trained for the same,
Each man born in the Island entered at youth to the
    game—
As it were almost cricket, not to be mastered in haste,
But after trial and labour, by temperance, living chaste.
As it were almost cricket—as it were even your play,
Weighed and pondered and worshipped, and practised day
    and day.
So ye shall bide sure-guarded when the restless lightnings
    wake
In the womb of the blotting war-cloud, and the pallid
    nations quake.
So, at the haggard trumpets, instant your soul shall leap
Forthright, accoutred, accepting—alert from the wells of
    sleep.

So at the threat ye shall summon—so at the need ye shall
     send

Men, not children or servants, tempered and taught to the
     end;

Cleansed of servile panic, slow to dread or despise,

Humble because of knowledge, mighty by sacrifice. . . .

But ye say, 'It will mar our comfort.' Ye say, 'It will
     minish our trade.'

Do ye wait for the spattered shrapnel ere ye learn how a
     gun is laid?

For the low, red glare to southward when the raided coast-
     towns burn?

(Light ye shall have on that lesson, but little time to learn.)

Will ye pitch some white pavilion, and lustily even the
     odds,

With nets and hoops and mallets, with rackets and bats
     and rods?

Will the rabbit war with your foemen—the red deer horn
     them for hire?

Your kept cock-pheasant keep you?—he is master of
     many a shire.

Arid, aloof, incurious, unthinking, unthanking, gelt,

Will ye loose your schools to flout them till their brow-
     beat columns melt?

Will ye pray them or preach them, or print them, or ballot
     them back from your shore?

Will your workmen issue a mandate to bid them strike no
     more?

Will ye rise and dethrone your rulers? (Because ye were
     idle both?

Pride by Insolence chastened? Indolence purged by
     Sloth?)

No doubt but ye are the People; who shall make you
     afraid?

Also your gods are many; no doubt but your gods shall
     aid.

Idols of greasy altars built for the body's ease;
Proud little brazen Baals and talking fetishes;
Teraphs of sept and party and wise wood-pavement
    gods—
These shall come down to the battle and snatch you from
    under the rods?
From the gusty, flickering gun-roll with viewless salvoes
    rent,
And the pitted hail of the bullets that tell not whence they
    were sent.
When ye are ringed as with iron, when ye are scourged as
    with whips,
When the meat is yet in your belly, and the boast is yet on
    your lips;
When ye go forth at morning and the noon beholds you
    broke,
Ere ye lie down at even, your remnant, under the yoke?

No doubt but ye are the People—absolute, strong, and
    wise;
Whatever your heart has desired ye have not withheld from
    your eyes.
On your own heads, in your own hands, the sin and the
    saving lies!

THE VETERANS

(*Written for the gathering of survivors of the Indian Mutiny,
Albert Hall, 1907*)

To-day, across our fathers' graves,
    The astonished years reveal
The remnants of that desperate host
    Which cleansed our East with steel.

Hail and farewell! We greet you here,
    With tears that none will scorn—
O Keepers of the House of old,
    Or ever we were born!

One service more we dare to ask—
    Pray for us, heroes, pray,
That when Fate lays on us our task
    We do not shame the Day!

THE DYKES
1902

We have no heart for the fishing—we have no hand for
    the oar—
All that our fathers taught us of old pleases us now no
    more.
All that our own hearts bid us believe we doubt where we
    do not deny—
There is no proof in the bread we eat nor rest in the toil
    we ply.

Look you, our foreshore stretches far through sea-gate,
    dyke, and groin—
Made land all, that our fathers made, where the flats and
    the fairway join.
They forced the sea a sea-league back. They died, and
    their work stood fast.
We were born to peace in the lee of the dykes, but the time
    of our peace is past.

Far off, the full tide clambers and slips, mouthing and
    testing all,
Nipping the flanks of the water-gates, baying along the
    wall;

133

Turning the shingle, returning the shingle, changing the
    set of the sand . . .
We are too far from the beach, men say, to know how the
    outworks stand.

So we come down, uneasy, to look; uneasily pacing the
    beach.
These are the dykes our fathers made: we have never
    known a breach.
Time and again has the gale blown by and we were not
    afraid;
Now we come only to look at the dykes—at the dykes our
    fathers made.

O'er the marsh where the homesteads cower apart the
    harried sunlight flies,
Shifts and considers, wanes and recovers, scatters and
    sickens and dies—
An evil ember bedded in ash—a spark blown west by the
    wind . . .
We are surrendered to night and the sea—the gale and the
    tide behind!

At the bridge of the lower saltings the cattle gather and
    blare,
Roused by the feet of running men, dazed by the lantern-
    glare.
Unbar and let them away for their lives—the levels drown
    as they stand,
Where the flood-wash forces the sluices aback and the
    ditches deliver inland.

Ninefold deep to the top of the dykes the galloping
    breakers stride,
And their overcarried spray is a sea—a sea on the land-
    ward side.

134

Coming, like stallions they paw with their hooves, going
   they snatch with their teeth,
Till the bents and the furze and the sand are dragged out,
   and the old-time hurdles beneath.

Bid men gather fuel for fire, the tar, the oil, and the tow—
Flame we shall need, not smoke, in the dark if the riddled
   sea-banks go.
Bid the ringers watch in the tower (who knows how the
   dawn shall prove?)
Each with his rope between his feet and the trembling bells
   above.

Now we can only wait till the day, wait and apportion our
   shame.
These are the dykes our fathers left, but we would not look
   to the same.
Time and again were we warned of the dykes, time and
   again we delayed:
Now, it may fall, we have slain our sons, as our fathers we
   have betrayed.

.   .   .   .   .

Walking along the wreck of the dykes, watching the work
   of the seas!
These were the dykes our fathers made to our great profit
   and ease.
But the peace is gone and the profit is gone, with the old
   sure days withdrawn . . .
That our own houses show as strange when we come back
   in the dawn!

135

THE WHITE MAN'S BURDEN

1899

(The United States and the Philippine Islands)

Take up the White Man's burden—
　Send forth the best ye breed —
Go bind your sons to exile
　To serve your captives' need;
To wait in heavy harness
　On fluttered folk and wild—
Your new-caught, sullen peoples,
　Half devil and half child.

Take up the White Man's burden—
　In patience to abide,
To veil the threat of terror
　And check the show of pride;
By open speech and simple,
　An hundred times made plain,
To seek another's profit,
　And work another's gain.

Take up the White Man's burden—
　The savage wars of peace—
Fill full the mouth of Famine
　And bid the sickness cease;
And when your goal is nearest
　The end for others sought,
Watch Sloth and heathen Folly
　Bring all your hope to nought.

Take up the White Man's burden—
　No tawdry rule of kings,
But toil of serf and sweeper—
　The tale of common things.

The ports ye shall not enter,
    The roads ye shall not tread,
Go make them with your living,
    And mark them with your dead!

Take up the White Man's burden—
    And reap his old reward:
The blame of those ye better,
    The hate of those ye guard—
The cry of hosts ye humour
    (Ah, slowly!) toward the light:—
'Why brought ye us from bondage,
    'Our loved Egyptian night?'

Take up the White Man's burden—
    Ye dare not stoop to less—
Nor call too loud on Freedom
    To cloak your weariness;
By all ye cry or whisper,
    By all ye leave or do,
The silent, sullen peoples
    Shall weigh your Gods and you.

Take up the White Man's burden—
    Have done with childish days—
The lightly proffered laurel,
    The easy, ungrudged praise.
Comes now, to search your manhood
    Through all the thankless years,
Cold-edged with dear-bought wisdom,
    The judgment of your peers!

HYMN BEFORE ACTION
1896

The earth is full of anger,
  The seas are dark with wrath,
The Nations in their harness
  Go up against our path:
Ere yet we loose the legions
  Ere yet we draw the blade,
Jehovah of the Thunders,
  Lord God of Battles, aid!

High lust and froward bearing,
  Proud heart, rebellious brow—
Deaf ear and soul uncaring,
  We seek Thy mercy now!
The sinner that forswore Thee,
  The fool that passed Thee by,
Our times are known before Thee—
  Lord, grant us strength to die!

For those who kneel beside us
  At altars not Thine own,
Who lack the lights that guide us,
  Lord, let their faith atone!
If wrong we did to call them,
  By honour bound they came;
Let not Thy Wrath befall them,
  But deal to us the blame.

From panic, pride, and terror,
  Revenge that knows no rein—
Light haste and lawless error,
  Protect us yet again.
Cloke Thou our undeserving,
  Make firm the shuddering breath,
In silence and unswerving
  To taste Thy lesser death.

Ah, Mary pierced with sorrow,
    Remember, reach and save
The soul that comes to-morrow
    Before the God that gave!
Since each was born of woman,
    For each at utter need—
True comrade and true foeman—
    Madonna, intercede!

E'en now their vanguard gathers,
    E'en now we face the fray—
As Thou didst help our fathers,
    Help Thou our host to-day.
Fulfilled of signs and wonders,
    In life, in death made clear—
Jehovah of the Thunders,
    Lord God of Battles, hear!

RECESSIONAL
1897

God of our fathers, known of old,
    Lord of our far-flung battle-line,
Beneath whose awful Hand we hold
    Dominion over palm and pine—
Lord God of Hosts, be with us yet,
Lest we forget—lest we forget!

The tumult and the shouting dies;
    The Captains and the Kings depart:
Still stands Thine ancient sacrifice,
    An humble and a contrite heart.

Lord God of Hosts, be with us yet,
Lest we forget—lest we forget!

Far-called, our navies melt away;
   On dune and headland sinks the fire:
Lo, all our pomp of yesterday
   Is one with Nineveh and Tyre!
Judge of the Nations, spare us yet,
Lest we forget—lest we forget!

If, drunk with sight of power, we loose
   Wild tongues that have not Thee in awe,
Such boastings as the Gentiles use,
   Or lesser breeds without the Law—
Lord God of Hosts, be with us yet,
Lest we forget—lest we forget!

For heathen heart that puts her trust
   In reeking tube and iron shard,
All valiant dust that builds on dust,
   And guarding, calls not Thee to guard.
For frantic boast and foolish word—
Thy mercy on Thy People, Lord!

'FOR ALL WE HAVE AND ARE'

1914

For all we have and are,
   For all our children's fate,
Stand up and take the war.
The Hun is at the gate!
Our world has passed away,
In wantonness o'erthrown.
There is nothing left to-day
But steel and fire and stone!

Though all we knew depart,
The old Commandments stand:—
'In courage keep your heart,
In strength lift up your hand.'

Once more we hear the word
That sickened earth of old:—
'No law except the Sword
Unsheathed and uncontrolled.'
Once more it knits mankind,
Once more the nations go
To meet and break and bind
A crazed and driven foe.

Comfort, content, delight,
The ages' slow-bought gain,
They shrivelled in a night.
Only ourselves remain
To face the naked days
In silent fortitude,
Through perils and dismays
Renewed and re-renewed.
    Though all we made depart,
    The old Commandments stand:—
    'In patience keep your heart,
    In strength lift up your hand.'

No easy hope or lies
Shall bring us to our goal,
But iron sacrifice
Of body, will, and soul.
There is but one task for all—
One life for each to give.
What stands if Freedom fall?
Who dies if England live?

141

THE BENEFACTORS

Ah! What avails the classic bent
  And what the cultured word,
Against the undoctored incident
  That actually occurred?

And what is Art whereto we press
  Through paint and prose and rhyme—
When Nature in her nakedness
  Defeats us every time?

It is not learning, grace nor gear,
  Nor easy meat and drink,
But bitter pinch of pain and fear
  That makes creation think.

When in this world's unpleasing youth
  Our godlike race began,
The longest arm, the sharpest tooth,
  Gave man control of man;

Till, bruised and bitten to the bone
  And taught by pain and fear,
He learned to deal the far-off stone,
  And poke the long, safe spear.

So tooth and nail were obsolete
  As means against a foe,
Till, bored by uniform defeat,
  Some genius built the bow.

Then stone and javelin proved as vain
  As old-time tooth and nail;
Till, spurred anew by fear and pain,
  Man fashioned coats of mail.

Then was there safety for the rich
   And danger for the poor,
Till someone mixed a powder which
   Redressed the scale once more.

Helmet and armour disappeared
   With sword and bow and pike,
And, when the smoke of battle cleared,
   All men were armed alike. . . .

And when ten million such were slain
   To please one crazy king,
Man, schooled in bulk by fear and pain,
   Grew weary of the thing;

And, at the very hour designed
   To enslave him past recall,
His tooth-stone-arrow-gun-shy mind
   Turned and abolished all.

All Power, each Tyrant, every Mob
   Whose head has grown too large,
Ends by destroying its own job
   And works its own discharge;

And Man, whose mere necessities
   Move all things from his path,
Trembles meanwhile at their decrees,
   And deprecates their wrath!

THE CRAFTSMAN

Once, after long-drawn revel at The Mermaid,
  He to the overbearing Boanerges
Jonson, uttered (if half of it were liquor,
      Blessed be the vintage!)

Saying how, at an alehouse under Cotswold,
He had made sure of his very Cleopatra
Drunk with enormous, salvation-contemning
              Love for a tinker.

How, while he hid from Sir Thomas's keepers,
Crouched in a ditch and drenched by the midnight
Dews, he had listened to gipsy Juliet
              Rail at the dawning.

How at Bankside, a boy drowning kittens
Winced at the business; whereupon his sister—
Lady Macbeth aged seven—thrust 'em under,
              Sombrely scornful.

How on a Sabbath, hushed and compassionate—
She being known since her birth to the townsfolk—
Stratford dredged and delivered from Avon
              Dripping Ophelia.

So, with a thin third finger marrying
Drop to wine-drop domed on the table,
Shakespeare opened his heart till the sunrise
              Entered to hear him.

London waked and he, imperturbable,
Passed from waking to hurry after shadows . . .
Busied upon shows of no earthly importance?
              Yes, but he knew it!

SAMUEL PEPYS
1933

Like as the Oak whose roots descend
  Through earth and stillness seeking food
Most apt to furnish in the end
  That dense, indomitable wood

Which, felled, may arm a seaward flank
  Of Ostia's mole or—bent to frame
The beaked Liburnian's triple bank—
  Carry afar the Roman name;

But which, a tree, the season moves
  Through gentler Gods than Wind or Tide,
Delightedly to harbour doves,
  Or take some clasping vine for bride;

So this man—prescient to ensure
  (Since even now his orders hold)
A little State might ride secure
  At sea from foes her sloth made bold,—

Turned in his midmost harried round,
  As Venus drove or Liber led,
And snatched from any shrine he found
  The Stolen Draught, the Secret Bread.

Nor these alone. His life betrayed
  No gust unslaked, no pleasure missed.
He called the obedient Nine to aid
  The varied chase. And Clio kissed;

Bidding him write each sordid love,
  Shame, panic, stratagem, and lie
In full, that sinners undiscov-
  ered, like ourselves, might say:—''Tis I!'

145

'WHEN 'OMER SMOTE 'IS BLOOMIN' LYRE'

(Introduction to the Barrack-Room Ballads in 'The Seven Seas')

When 'Omer smote 'is bloomin' lyre,
    He'd 'eard men sing by land an' sea;
An' what he thought 'e might require,
    'E went an' took—the same as me!

The market-girls an' fishermen,
    The shepherds an' the sailors, too,
They 'eard old songs turn up again,
    But kep' it quiet—same as you!

They knew 'e stole; 'e knew they knowed.
    They didn't tell, nor make a fuss,
But winked at 'Omer down the road,
    An' 'e winked back—the same as us!

TOMLINSON

1891

Now Tomlinson gave up the ghost at his house in
    Berkeley Square,
And a Spirit came to his bedside and gripped him by the
    hair—
A Spirit gripped him by the hair and carried him far away,
Till he heard as the roar of a rain-fed ford the roar of the
    Milky Way:
Till he heard the roar of the Milky Way die down and
    drone and cease,
And they came to the Gate within the Wall where Peter
    holds the keys.

'Stand up, stand up now, Tomlinson, and answer loud and
   high
'The good that ye did for the sake of men or ever ye came
   to die—
'The good that ye did for the sake of men on little Earth
   so lone!'
And the naked soul of Tomlinson grew white as a rain-
   washed bone.
'O I have a friend on Earth,' he said, 'that was my priest
   and guide,
'And well would he answer all for me if he were at my
   side.'
—'For that ye strove in neighbour-love it shall be written
   fair,
'But now ye wait at Heaven's Gate and not in Berkeley
   Square:
'Though we called your friend from his bed this night, he
   could not speak for you,
'For the race is run by one and one and never by two and
   two.'
Then Tomlinson looked up and down, and little gain was
   there,
For the naked stars grinned overhead, and he saw that his
   soul was bare.
The Wind that blows between the Worlds, it cut him like
   a knife,
And Tomlinson took up the tale and spoke of his good in
   life.
'O this I have read in a book,' he said, 'and that was told
   to me,
'And this I have thought that another man thought of a
   Prince in Muscovy.'
The good souls flocked like homing doves and bade him
   clear the path,
And Peter twirled the jangling Keys in weariness and
   wrath.

147

'Ye have read, ye have heard, ye have thought,' he said,
    'and the tale is yet to run:
'By the worth of the body that once ye had, give answer—
    what ha' ye done?'
Then Tomlinson looked back and forth, and little good it
    bore,
For the darkness stayed at his shoulder-blade and Heaven's
    Gate before:—
'O this I have felt, and this I have guessed, and this I have
    heard men say,
'And this they wrote that another man wrote of a carl in
    Norroway.'
'Ye have read, ye have felt, ye have guessed, good lack!
    Ye have hampered Heaven's Gate;
'There's little room between the stars in idleness to prate!
'For none may reach by hired speech of neighbour, prie st
    and kin
'Through borrowed deed to God's good meed that lies so
    fair within;
'Get hence, get hence to the Lord of Wrong, for the doom
    has yet to run,
'And . . . the faith that ye share with Berkeley Square
    uphold you, Tomlinson!'
    .   .   .   .   .

The Spirit gripped him by the hair, and sun by sun they
    fell
Till they came to the belt of Naughty Stars that rim the
    mouth of Hell.
The first are red with pride and wrath, the next are white
    with pain,
But the third are black with clinkered sin that cannot burn
    again.
They may hold their path, they may leave their path, with
    never a soul to mark:
They may burn or freeze, but they must not cease in the
    Scorn of the Outer Dark.

The Wind that blows between the Worlds, it nipped him
to the bone,
And he yearned to the flare of Hell-gate there as the light
of his own hearth-stone.
The Devil he sat behind the bars, where the desperate
legions drew,
But he caught the hasting Tomlinson and would not let
him through.
'Wot ye the price of good pit-coal that I must pay?' said
he,
'That ye rank yoursel' so fit for Hell and ask no leave of
me?
'I am all o'er-sib to Adam's breed that ye should give me
scorn,
'For I strove with God for your First Father the day that
he was born.
'Sit down, sit down upon the slag, and answer loud and
high
'The harm that ye did to the Sons of Men or ever you came
to die.'
And Tomlinson looked up and up, and saw against the
night
The belly of a tortured star blood-red in Hell-Mouth
light;
And Tomlinson looked down and down, and saw beneath
his feet
The frontlet of a tortured star milk-white in Hell-Mouth
heat.
'O I had a love on earth,' said he, 'that kissed me to my
fall;
'And if ye would call my love to me I know she would
answer all.'
—'All that ye did in love forbid it shall be written
fair,
'But now ye wait at Hell-Mouth Gate and not in Berkeley
Square;

149

'Though we whistled your love from her bed to-night, I
  trow she would not run,
'For the sin ye do by two and two ye must pay for one by
  one!'
The Wind that blows between the Worlds, it cut him like a
  knife,
And Tomlinson took up the tale and spoke of his sins in
  life:—
'Once I ha' laughed at the power of Love and twice at the
  grip of the Grave,
'And thrice I ha' patted my God on the head that men
  might call me brave.'
The Devil he blew on a brandered soul and set it aside to
  cool:—
'Do ye think I would waste my good pit-coal on the hide
  of a brain-sick fool?
'I see no worth in the hobnailed mirth or the jolthead jest
  ye did
'That I should waken my gentlemen that are sleeping three
  on a grid.'
Then Tomlinson looked back and forth, and there was
  little grace,
For Hell-Gate filled the houseless soul with the Fear of
  Naked Space.
'Nay, this I ha' heard,' quo' Tomlinson, 'and this was
  noised abroad,
'And this I ha' got from a Belgian book on the word of a
  dead French lord.'
—'Ye ha' heard, ye ha' read, ye ha' got, good lack! and
  the tale begins afresh—
'Have ye sinned one sin for the pride o' the eye or the
  sinful lust of the flesh?'
Then Tomlinson he gripped the bars and yammered, 'Let
  me in—
'For I mind that I borrowed my neighbour's wife to sin
  the deadly sin.'

150

The Devil he grinned behind the bars, and banked the fires
high:
'Did ye read of that sin in a book?' said he; and Tomlin-
son said, 'Ay!'
The Devil he blew upon his nails, and the little devils
ran,
And he said: 'Go husk this whimpering thief that comes
in the guise of a man:
'Winnow him out 'twixt star and star, and sieve his proper
worth:
'There's sore decline in Adam's line if this be spawn of
Earth.'
Empusa's crew, so naked-new they may not face the
fire,
But weep that they bin too small to sin to the height of
their desire,
Over the coal they chased the Soul, and racked it all
abroad,
As children rifle a caddis-case or the raven's foolish
hoard.
And back they came with the tattered Thing, as children
after play,
And they said: 'The soul that he got from God he has
bartered clean away.
'We have threshed a stook of print and book, and win-
nowed a chattering wind,
'And many a soul wherefrom he stole, but his we cannot
find.
'We have handled him, we have dandled him, we have
seared him to the bone,
'And, Sire, if tooth and nail show truth he has no soul of
his own.'
The Devil he bowed his head on his breast and rumbled
deep and low:—
'I'm all o'er-sib to Adam's breed that I should bid him
go.

151

'Yet close we lie, and deep we lie, and if I gave him place,

'My gentlemen that are so proud would flout me to my face;

'They'd call my house a common stews and me a careless host,

'And—I would not anger my gentlemen for the sake of a shiftless ghost.'

The Devil he looked at the mangled Soul that prayed to feel the flame,

And he thought of Holy Charity, but he thought of his own good name:—

'Now ye could haste my coal to waste, and sit ye down to fry.

'Did ye think of that theft for yourself?' said he; and Tomlinson said, 'Ay!'

The Devil he blew an outward breath, for his heart was free from care:—

'Ye have scarce the soul of a louse,' he said, 'but the roots of sin are there,

'And for that sin should ye come in were I the lord alone,

'But sinful pride has rule inside—ay, mightier than my own.

'Honour and Wit, fore-damned they sit, to each his Priest and Whore;

'Nay, scarce I dare myself go there, and you they'd torture sore.

'Ye are neither spirit nor spirk,' he said; 'ye are neither book nor brute—

'Go, get ye back to the flesh again for the sake of Man's repute.

'I'm all o'er-sib to Adam's breed that I should mock your pain,

'But look that ye win to worthier sin ere ye come back again.

152

'Get hence, the hearse is at your door—the grim black
stallions wait—
'They bear your clay to place to-day. Speed, lest ye come
too late!
'Go back to Earth with a lip unsealed—go back with an
open eye,
'And carry my word to the Sons of Men or ever ye come
to die:
'That the sin they do by two and two they must pay for
one by one,
'And . . . the God that you took from a printed book
be with you, Tomlinson!'

THE LAST RHYME OF TRUE THOMAS
1893

The King has called for priest and cup,
  The King has taken spur and blade
To dub True Thomas a belted knight,
  And all for the sake of the songs he made.

They have sought him high, they have sought
  him low,
  They have sought him over down and lea.
They have found him by the milk-white thorn
  That guards the Gates of Faerie.

'Twas bent beneath and blue above :
  Their eyes were held that they might not see
The kine that grazed beneath the knowes,
  Oh, they were the Queens of Faerie!

'Now cease your song,' the King he said,
  'Oh, cease your song and get you dight
'To vow your vow and watch your arms,
  'For I will dub you a belted knight.

'For I will give you a horse o' pride,
  'Wi' blazon and spur and page and squire;
'Wi' keep and tail and seizin and law,
  'And land to hold at your desire.'

True Thomas smiled above his harp,
  And turned his face to the naked sky,
Where, blown before the wastrel wind,
  The thistle-down she floated by.

'I ha' vowed my vow in another place,
  'And bitter oath it was on me.
'I ha' watched my arms the lee-long night,
  'Where five-score fighting men would flee.

'My lance is tipped o' the hammered flame,
  'My shield is beat o' the moonlight cold;
'And I won my spurs in the Middle World,
  'A thousand fathom beneath the mould.

'And what should I make wi' a horse o' pride,
  'And what should I make wi' a sword so brown,
'But spill the rings of the Gentle Folk
  'And flyte my kin in the Fairy Town?

'And what should I make wi' blazon and belt,
  'Wi' keep and tail and seizin and fee,
'And what should I do wi' page and squire
  'That am a king in my own countrie?

'For I send east and I send west,
  'And I send far as my will may flee,
'By dawn and dusk and the drinking rain,
  'And syne my Sendings return to me.

'They come wi' news of the groanin' earth,
  'They come wi' news of the roarin' sea.
'Wi' word of Spirit and Ghost and Flesh,
  'And man, that's mazed among the three.'

The King he bit his nether lip,
  And smote his hand upon his knee:
'By the faith of my soul, True Thomas,' he said,
  'Ye waste no wit in courtesie!

'As I desire, unto my pride,
  'Can I make Earls by three and three,
'To run before and ride behind
  'And serve the sons o' my body.'

'And what care I for your row-foot earls,
  'Or all the sons o' your body?
'Before they win to the Pride o' Name,
  'I trow they all ask leave o' me.

'For I make Honour wi' muckle mouth,
  'As I make Shame wi' mincing feet,
'To sing wi' the priests at the market-cross,
  'Or run wi' the dogs in the naked street.

'And some they give me the good red gold,
  'And some they give me the white money,
'And some they give me a clout o' meal,
  'For they be people of low degree.

'And the song I sing for the counted gold
  'The same I sing for the white money,
'But best I sing for the clout o' meal,
  'That simple people given me.'

The King cast down a silver groat,
  A silver groat o' Scots money,
'If I come wi' a poor man's dole,' he said,
  'True Thomas, will ye harp to me?'

'Whenas I harp to the children small,
  'They press me close on either hand.
'And who are you,' True Thomas said,
  'That you should ride while they must stand?

'Light down, light down from your horse o' pride.
  'I trow ye talk too loud and hie,
'And I will make you a triple word,
  'And syne, if ye dare, ye shall 'noble me.'

He has lighted down from his horse o' pride,
  And set his back against a stone.
'Now guard you well,' True Thomas said,
  'Ere I rax your heart from your breast-bone!'

True Thomas played upon his harp,
  The fairy harp that couldna lee,
And the first least word the proud King heard,
  It harpit the salt tear out o' his e'e.

'Oh, I see the love that I lost long syne,
  'I touch the hope that I may not see,
'And all that I did of hidden shame,
  'Like little snakes they hiss at me.

156

'The sun is lost at noon —at noon!
    'The dread of doom has grippit me.
'True Thomas, hide me under your cloak,
    'God wot, I'm little fit to dee!'

'Twas bent beneath and blue above—
    'Twas open field and running flood—
Where, hot on heath and dyke and wall,
    The high sun warmed the adder's brood.

'Lie down, lie down,' True Thomas said.
    'The God shall judge when all is done,
'But I will bring you a better word
    'And lift the cloud that I laid on.'

True Thomas played upon his harp,
    That birled and brattled to his hand,
And the next least word True Thomas made
    It garred the King take horse and brand.

'Oh, I hear the tread o' the fighting-men,
    'I see the sun on splent and spear.
'I mark the arrow outen the fern
    'That flies so low and sings so clear!

'Advance my standards to that war,
    'And bid my good knights prick and ride
'The gled shall watch as fierce a fight
    'As e'er was fought on the Border-side!'

'Twas bent beneath and blue above,
    'Twas nodding grass and naked sky,
Where, ringing up the wastrel wind,
    The eyass stooped upon the pye.

157

True Thomas sighed above his harp,
　　And turned the song on the midmost string;
And the last least word True Thomas made,
　　He harpit his dead youth back to the King.

'Now I am prince, and I do well
　　'To love my love withouten fear;
'To walk with man in fellowship,
　　'And breathe my horse behind the deer.

'My hounds they bay unto the death,
　　'The buck has couched beyond the burn,
'My love she waits at her window
　　'To wash my hands when I return.

'For that I live am I content
　　'(Oh! I have seen my true love's eyes)
'To stand with Adam in Eden-glade,
　　'And run in the woods o' Paradise!'

'Twas naked sky and nodding grass,
　　'Twas running flood and wastrel wind,
Where, checked against the open pass,
　　The red deer turned to wait the hind.

True Thomas laid his harp away,
　　And louted low at the saddle-side;
He has taken stirrup and hauden rein,
　　And set the King on his horse o' pride.

'Sleep ye or wake,' True Thomas said,
　　'That sit so still, that muse so long?
'Sleep ye or wake?—till the Latter Sleep
　　'I trow ye'll not forget my song.

'I ha' harpit a Shadow out o' the sun
  'To stand before your face and cry;
'I ha' armed the earth beneath your heel,
  'And over your head I ha' dusked the sky.

'I ha' harpit ye up to the Throne o' God,
  'I ha' harpit your midmost soul in three.
'I ha' harpit ye down to the Hinges o' Hell,
  'And—ye—would—make—a Knight o' me!'

THE SONS OF MARTHA
1907

The Sons of Mary seldom bother, for they have inherited
    that good part;
But the Sons of Martha favour their Mother of the careful
    soul and the troubled heart.
And because she lost her temper once, and because she was
    rude to the Lord her Guest,
Her Sons must wait upon Mary's Sons, world without end,
    reprieve, or rest.

It is their care in all the ages to take the buffet and cushion
    the shock.
It is their care that the gear engages; it is their care that the
    switches lock.
It is their care that the wheels run truly; it is their care to
    embark and entrain,
Tally, transport, and deliver duly the Sons of Mary by
    land and main.

They say to mountains, 'Be ye removèd.' They say to the
    lesser floods, 'Be dry.'
Under their rods are the rocks reprovèd—they are not
    afraid of that which is high.

159

Then do the hill-tops shake to the summit—then is the bed
of the deep laid bare,
That the Sons of Mary may overcome it, pleasantly sleep-
ing and unaware.

They finger death at their gloves' end where they piece and
repiece the living wires.
He rears against the gates they tend: they feed him hungry
behind their fires.
Early at dawn, ere men see clear, they stumble into his
terrible stall,
And hale him forth like a haltered steer, and goad and turn
him till evenfall.

To these from birth is Belief forbidden; from these till
death is Relief afar.
They are concerned with matters hidden—under the earth-
line their altars are—
The secret fountains to follow up, waters withdrawn to
restore to the mouth,
And gather the floods as in a cup, and pour them again at
a city's drouth.

They do not preach that their God will rouse them a little
before the nuts work loose.
They do not teach that His Pity allows them to drop their
job when they dam'-well choose.
As in the thronged and the lighted ways, so in the dark and
the desert they stand,
Wary and watchful all their days that their brethren's days
may be long in the land.

Raise ye the stone or cleave the wood to make a path more
fair or flat—
Lo, it is black already with blood some Son of Martha
spilled for that!

Not as a ladder from earth to Heaven, not as a witness to
  any creed,
But simple service simply given to his own kind in their
  common need.

And the Sons of Mary smile and are blessèd—they know
  the Angels are on their side.
They know in them is the Grace confessèd, and for them
  are the Mercies multiplied.
They sit at the Feet—they hear the Word—they see how
  truly the Promise runs.
They have cast their burden upon the Lord, and—the Lord
  He lays it on Martha's Sons!

EPITAPHS OF THE WAR
1914–18

'EQUALITY OF SACRIFICE'

A. 'I was a Have.' *B.* 'I was a "have-not."'
  (*Together.*) 'What hast thou given which I gave
  not?'

A SERVANT

We were together since the War began.
He was my servant—and the better man.

A SON

My son was killed while laughing at some jest. I would I
  knew
What it was, and it might serve me in a time when jests are
  few.

AN ONLY SON

I have slain none except my Mother. She
(Blessing her slayer) died of grief for me.

161

EX-CLERK

Pity not! The Army gave
Freedom to a timid slave:
In which Freedom did he find
Strength of body, will, and mind:
By which strength he came to prove
Mirth, Companionship, and Love:
For which Love to Death he went:
In which Death he lies content.

THE WONDER

Body and Spirit I surrendered whole
To harsh Instructors—and received a soul . . .
If mortal man could change me through and through
From all I was—what may The God not do?

HINDU SEPOY IN FRANCE

This man in his own country prayed we know not to what
    Powers.
We pray Them to reward him for his bravery in ours.

THE COWARD

I could not look on Death, which being known,
Men led me to him, blindfold and alone.

SHOCK

My name, my speech, my self I had forgot.
My wife and children came—I knew them not.
I died. My Mother followed. At her call
And on her bosom I remembered all.

A GRAVE NEAR CAIRO

Gods of the Nile, should this stout fellow here
Get out—get out! He knows not shame nor fear.

PELICANS IN THE WILDERNESS
A Grave near Halfa

The blown sand heaps on me, that none may learn
   Where I am laid for whom my children grieve. . . .
O wings that beat at dawning, ye return
   Out of the desert to your young at eve!

TWO CANADIAN MEMORIALS

I

We giving all gained all.
   Neither lament us nor praise.
Only in all things recall,
   It is Fear, not Death, that slays.

II

From little towns in a far land we came,
   To save our honour and a world aflame.
By little towns in a far land we sleep;
   And trust that world we won for you to keep!

THE FAVOUR

Death favoured me from the first, well knowing I could not
   endure
  To wait on him day by day. He quitted my betters and
   came
Whistling over the fields, and, when he had made all sure,
  'Thy line is at end,' he said, 'but at least I have saved its
   name.'

THE BEGINNER

On the first hour of my first day
   In the front trench I fell.
(Children in boxes at a play
   Stand up to watch it well.)

R.A.F. (AGED EIGHTEEN)

Laughing through clouds, his milk-teeth still unshed,
Cities and men he smote from overhead.
His deaths delivered, he returned to play
Childlike, with childish things now put away.

THE REFINED MAN

I was of delicate mind. I stepped aside for my needs,
    Disdaining the common office. I was seen from afar and
        killed. . . .
How is this matter for mirth? Let each man be judged by
        his deeds.
    *I have paid my price to live with myself on the terms that I
        willed.*

NATIVE WATER-CARRIER (M.E.F.)

Prometheus brought down fire to men.
    This brought up water.
The Gods are jealous—now, as then,
    Giving no quarter.

THE SLEEPY SENTINEL

Faithless the watch that I kept: now I have none to keep.
I was slain because I slept: now I am slain I sleep.
Let no man reproach me again, whatever watch is unkept—
I sleep because I am slain. They slew me because I slept.

BATTERIES OUT OF AMMUNITION

If any mourn us in the workshop, say
We died because the shift kept holiday.

COMMON FORM

If any question why we died,
Tell them, because our fathers lied.

164

A DEAD STATESMAN

I could not dig: I dared not rob:
Therefore I lied to please the mob.
Now all my lies are proved untrue
And I must face the men I slew.
What tale shall serve me here among
Mine angry and defrauded young?

THE REBEL

If I had clamoured at Thy Gate
    For gift of Life on Earth,
And, thrusting through the souls that wait,
    Flung headlong into birth—
Even then, even then, for gin and snare
    About my pathway spread,
Lord, I had mocked Thy thoughtful care
    Before I joined the Dead!
But now? . . . I was beneath Thy Hand
    Ere yet the Planets came.
And now—though Planets pass, I stand
    The witness to Thy shame!

THE OBEDIENT

Daily, though no ears attended,
    Did my prayers arise.
Daily, though no fire descended,
    Did I sacrifice.
Though my darkness did not lift,
    Though I faced no lighter odds,
Though the Gods bestowed no gift,
            None the less,
  None the less, I served the Gods!

165

A DRIFTER OFF TARENTUM

He from the wind-bitten North with ship and companions
    descended,
  Searching for eggs of death spawned by invisible hulls.
Many he found and drew forth. Of a sudden the fishery
    ended
  In flame and a clamorous breath known to the eye-
    pecking gulls.

DESTROYERS IN COLLISION

  For Fog and Fate no charm is found
    To lighten or amend.
  I, hurrying to my bride, was drowned—
    Cut down by my best friend.

CONVOY ESCORT

  I was a shepherd to fools
    Causelessly bold or afraid.
  They would not abide by my rules.
    Yet they escaped. For I stayed.

UNKNOWN FEMALE CORPSE

  Headless, lacking foot and hand,
  Horrible I come to land.
  I beseech all women's sons
  Know I was a mother once.

RAPED AND REVENGED

One used and butchered me: another spied
Me broken—for which thing an hundred died.
So it was learned among the heathen hosts
How much a freeborn woman's favour costs.

166

SALONIKAN GRAVE

I have watched a thousand days
Push out and crawl into night
Slowly as tortoises.
Now I, too, follow these.
It is fever, and not the fight—
Time, not battle,—that slays.

THE BRIDEGROOM

Call me not false, beloved,
    If, from thy scarce-known breast
So little time removed,
    In other arms I rest.

For this more ancient bride,
    Whom coldly I embrace,
Was constant at my side
    Before I saw thy face.

Our marriage, often set—
    By miracle delayed—
At last is consummate,
    And cannot be unmade.

Live, then, whom Life shall cure,
    Almost, of Memory,
And leave us to endure
    Its immortality.

V.A.D. (MEDITERRANEAN)

Ah, would swift ships had never been, for then we ne'er
    had found,
These harsh Ægean rocks between, this little virgin
    drowned,

167

Whom neither spouse nor child shall mourn, but men she
    nursed through pain
And—certain keels for whose return the heathen look in
    vain.

ACTORS

*On a Memorial Tablet in Holy Trinity Church,
Stratford-on-Avon*

We counterfeited once for your disport
    Men's joy and sorrow: but our day has passed.
We pray you pardon all where we fell short—
    Seeing we were your servants to this last.

JOURNALISTS

On a Panel in the Hall of the Institute of Journalists
We have served our day.

'BOBS'

1898

*(Field-Marshal Lord Roberts of Kandahar : died in
France 1914)*

There's a little red-faced man,
    Which is Bobs,
Rides the tallest 'orse 'e can—
    Our Bobs.
If it bucks or kicks or rears,
'E can sit for twenty years
With a smile round both 'is ears—
    Can't yer, Bobs?

Then 'ere's to Bobs Bahadur—little Bobs, Bobs, Bobs!
'E's our pukka Kandaharder—
        Fightin' Bobs, Bobs, Bobs!
'E's the Dook of *Aggy Chel;*[1]
'E's the man that done us well,
An' we'll follow 'im to 'ell—
        Won't we, Bobs?

If a limber's slipped a trace,
        'Ook on Bobs.
If a marker's lost 'is place,
        Dress by Bobs.
For 'e's eyes all up 'is coat,
An' a bugle in 'is throat,
An' you will not play the goat
        Under Bobs.

'E's a little down on drink,
        Chaplain Bobs;
But it keeps us outer Clink—
        Don't it, Bobs?
So we will not complain
Tho' 'e's water on the brain,
If 'e leads us straight again—
        Blue-light[2] Bobs.

If you stood 'im on 'is head,
        Father Bobs,
You could spill a quart of lead
        Outer Bobs.
'E's been at it thirty years,
An' amassin' souveneers
In the way o' slugs an' spears—
        Ain't yer, Bobs?

[1] Get ahead.   [2] Temperance

What 'e does not know o' war,
>> Gen'ral Bobs,
You can arst the shop next door—
>> Can't they, Bobs?
Oh, 'e's little but he's wise,
'E's a terror for 'is size,
An'—'e—does—not—advertise—
>> Do yer, Bobs?

Now they've made a bloomin' Lord
>> Outer Bobs,
Which was but 'is fair reward—
>> Weren't it, Bobs?
So 'e'll wear a coronet
Where 'is 'elmet used to set;
But we know you won't forget—
>> Will yer, Bobs?

Then 'ere's to Bobs Bahadur—little Bobs, Bobs, Bobs,
Pocket-Wellin'ton an' *arder*[1]—
>> Fightin' Bobs, Bobs, Bobs!
This ain't no bloomin' ode,
But you've 'elped the soldier's load,
An' for benefits bestowed,
>> Bless yer, Bobs!

DANNY DEEVER

'What are the bugles blowin' for?' said Files-on-
>> Parade.
'To turn you out, to turn you out,' the Colour-Sergeant
>> said.

[1] And a half.

170

'What makes you look so white, so white?' said Files-on-
  Parade.
'I'm dreadin' what I've got to watch,' the Colour-Sergeant
  said.
  For they're hangin' Danny Deever, you can hear the
    Dead March play,
  The Regiment's in 'ollow square—they're hangin' him
    to-day;
  They've taken of his buttons off an' cut his stripes
    away,
  An' they're hangin' Danny Deever in the mornin'.

'What makes the rear-rank breathe so 'ard?' said Files-on-
  Parade.
'It's bitter cold, it's bitter cold,' the Colour-Sergeant
  said.
'What makes that front-rank man fall down?' said Files-
  on-Parade.
'A touch o' sun, a touch o' sun,' the Colour-Sergeant
  said.
  They are hangin' Danny Deever, they are marchin' of
    'im round,
  They 'ave 'alted Danny Deever by 'is coffin on the
    ground;
  An' 'e'll swing in 'arf a minute for a sneakin' shootin'
    hound—
  O they're hangin' Danny Deever in the mornin'!

''Is cot was right-'and cot to mine,' said Files-on-
  Parade.
''E's sleepin' out an' far to-night,' the Colour-Sergeant
  said.
'I've drunk 'is beer a score o' times,' said Files-on-
  Parade.
''E's drinkin' bitter beer alone,' the Colour-Sergeant
  said.

171

They are hangin' Danny Deever, you must mark 'im
    to 'is place,
For 'e shot a comrade sleepin'—you must look 'im in
    the face;
Nine 'undred of 'is county an' the Regiment's disgrace,
While they're hangin' Danny Deever in the mornin'.

'What's that so black agin the sun?' said Files-on-Parade.
'It's Danny fightin' 'ard for life,' the Colour-Sergeant said.
'What's that that whimpers over'ead?' said Files-on-
    Parade.
'It's Danny's soul that's passin' now,' the Colour-Sergeant
    said.
For they're done with Danny Deever, you can 'ear the
    quickstep play,
The Regiment's in column, an' they're marchin' us
    away;
Ho! the young recruits are shakin', an' they'll want
    their beer to-day,
After hangin' Danny Deever in the mornin'!

TOMMY

I went into a public-'ouse to get a pint o' beer,
  The publican 'e up an' sez, 'We serve no red-coats here.'
The girls be'ind the bar they laughed an' giggled fit to die,
I outs into the street again an' to myself sez I :
    O it's Tommy this, an' Tommy that, an' 'Tommy, go
      away';
    But it's 'Thank you, Mister Atkins,' when the band
      begins to play—
    The band begins to play, my boys, the band begins to
      play,
    O it's 'Thank you, Mister Atkins,' when the band
      begins to play.

I went into a theatre as sober as could be,
They gave a drunk civilian room, but 'adn't none for me;
They sent me to the gallery or round the music-'alls,
But when it comes to fightin', Lord! they'll shove me in
      the stalls!
      For it's Tommy this, an' Tommy that, an' 'Tommy,
            wait outside';
      But it's 'Special train for Atkins' when the trooper's
            on the tide—
      The troopship's on the tide, my boys, the troopship's
            on the tide,
      O it's 'Special train for Atkins' when the trooper's on
            the tide.

Yes, makin' mock o' uniforms that guard you while you
      sleep
Is cheaper than them uniforms, an' they're starvation
      cheap;
An' hustlin' drunken soldiers when they're goin' large a
      bit
Is five times better business than paradin' in full kit.
      Then it's Tommy this, an' Tommy that, an' 'Tommy,
            'ow's yer soul?'
      But it's 'Thin red line of 'eroes' when the drums begin
            to roll—
      The drums begin to roll, my boys, the drums begin to
            roll,
      O it's 'Thin red line of 'eroes' when the drums begin
            to roll.

We aren't no thin red 'eroes, nor we aren't no blackguards
      too,
But single men in barricks, most remarkable like you;
An' if sometimes our conduck isn't all your fancy paints,
Why, single men in barricks don't grow into plaster
      saints;

While it's Tommy this, an' Tommy that, an' 'Tommy,
        fall be'ind,'
But it's 'Please to walk in front, sir,' when there's
        trouble in the wind—
There's trouble in the wind, my boys, there's trouble
        in the wind,
O it's 'Please to walk in front, sir,' when there's
        trouble in the wind.

You talk o' better food for us, an' schools, an' fires, an'
        all:
We'll wait for extry rations if you treat us rational.
Don't mess about the cook-room slops, but prove it to our
        face
The Widow's Uniform is not the soldier-man's disgrace.
        For it's Tommy this, an' Tommy that, an' 'Chuck
                him out, the brute!'
        But it's 'Saviour of 'is country' when the guns begin
                to shoot;
        An' it's Tommy this, an' Tommy that, an' anything
                you please;
        An' Tommy ain't a bloomin' fool—you bet that
                Tommy sees!

'FUZZY-WUZZY'

(Soudan Expeditionary Force.   Early Campaigns)

We've fought with many men acrost the seas,
    An' some of 'em was brave an' some was not:
The Paythan an' the Zulu an' Burmese;
    But the Fuzzy was the finest o' the lot.
We never got a ha'porth's change of 'im:
    'E squatted in the scrub an' 'ocked our 'orses,
'E cut our sentries up at Sua*kim*,
    An' 'e played the cat an' banjo with our forces.

174

So 'ere's *to* you, Fuzzy-Wuzzy, at your 'ome in the
  Soudan ;
You're a pore benighted 'eathen but a first-class
  fightin' man;
We gives you your certificate, an' if you want it
  signed
We'll come an' 'ave a romp with you whenever you're
  inclined.

We took our chanst among the Kyber 'ills,
  The Boers knocked us silly at a mile,
The Burman give us Irriwaddy chills,
  An' a Zulu *impi* dished us up in style:
But all we ever got from such as they
  Was pop to what the Fuzzy made us swaller;
We 'eld our bloomin' own, the papers say,
  But man for man the Fuzzy knocked us 'oller.
    Then 'ere's *to* you, Fuzzy-Wuzzy, an' the missis and
      the kid ;
    Our orders was to break you, an' of course we went
      an' did.
    We sloshed you with Martinis, an' it wasn't 'ardly
      fair ;
    But for all the odds agin' you, Fuzzy-Wuz, you
      broke the square.

'E 'asn't got no papers of 'is own,
  'E 'asn't got no medals nor rewards,
So *we* must certify the skill 'e's shown
  In usin' of 'is long two-'anded swords:
When 'e's 'oppin' in an' out among the bush
  With 'is coffin-'eaded shield an' shovel-spear,
An 'appy day with Fuzzy on the rush
  Will last an 'ealthy Tommy for a year.

175

So 'ere's *to* you, Fuzzy-Wuzzy, an' your friends which
    are no more,
If we 'adn't lost some messmates we would 'elp you to
    deplore.
But give an' take's the gospel, an' we'll call the bargain
    fair,
For if you 'ave lost more than us, you crumpled up
    the square!

'E rushes at the smoke when we let drive,
    An' before we know, 'e's 'ackin' at our 'ead;
'E's all 'ot sand an' ginger when alive,
    An' 'e's generally shammin' when 'e's dead.
'E's a daisy, 'e's a ducky, 'e's a lamb!
    'E's a injia-rubber idiot on the spree,
'E's the on'y thing that doesn't give a damn
    For a Regiment o' British Infantree!
        So 'ere's *to* you, Fuzzy-Wuzzy, at your 'ome in the
            Soudan;
        You're a pore benighted 'eathen but a first-class
            fightin' man;
        An' 'ere's *to* you, Fuzzy-Wuzzy, with your 'ayrick 'ead
            of 'air—
        You big black boundin' beggar—for you broke a
            British square!

SCREW-GUNS

Smokin' my pipe on the mountings, sniffin' the mornin'-
    cool,
I walks in my old brown gaiters along o' my old brown
    mule,

With seventy gunners be'ind me, an' never a beggar forgets
It's only the pick of the Army that handles the dear little
pets—'Tss! 'Tss!
For you all love the screw-guns—the screw-guns they
all love you!
So when we call round with a few guns, o' course you
will know what to do—hoo! hoo!
Jest send in your Chief an' surrender—it's worse if
you fights or you runs:
You can go where you please, you can skid up the
trees, but you don't get away from the guns!

They sends us along where the roads are, but mostly we
goes where they ain't.
We'd climb up the side of a sign-board an' trust to the stick
o' the paint:
We've chivied the Naga an' Looshai; we've give the Afree-
deeman fits;
For we fancies ourselves at two thousand, we guns that
are built in two bits—'Tss! 'Tss!
For you all love the screw-guns . . .

If a man doesn't work, why, we drills 'im an' teaches 'im
'ow to behave.
If a beggar can't march, why, we kills 'im an' rattles 'im
into 'is grave.
You've got to stand up to our business an' spring without
snatchin' or fuss.
D'you say that you sweat with the field-guns? By God,
you must lather with us—'Tss! 'Tss!
For you all love the screw-guns . . .

The eagles is screamin' around us, the river's a-moanin'
below,
We're clear o' the pine an' the oak-scrub, we're out on the
rocks an' the snow,

177

An' the wind is as thin as a whip-lash what carries away
  to the plains
The rattle an' stamp o' the lead-mules—the jinglety-jink
  o' the chains—'Tss! 'Tss!
  For you all love the screw-guns . . .

There's a wheel on the Horns o' the Mornin', an' a wheel
  on the edge o' the Pit,
An' a drop into nothin' beneath you as straight as a beggar
  can spit:
With the sweat runnin' out o' your shirt-sleeves, an' the
  sun off the snow in your face,
An' 'arf o' the men on the drag-ropes to hold the old gun
  in 'er place—'Tss! 'Tss!
  For you all love the screw-guns . . .

Smokin' my pipe on the mountings, sniffin' the mornin'-
  cool,
I climbs in my old brown gaiters along o' my old brown
  mule.
The monkey can say what our road was—the wild-goat 'e
  knows where we passed.
Stand easy, you long-eared old darlin's! Out drag-
  ropes!
    With shrapnel! Hold fast—'Tss! 'Tss!
  For you all love the screw-guns—the screw-guns they
    all love you!
  So when we take tea with a few guns, o' course you
    will know what to do—hoo! hoo!
  Jest send in your Chief an' surrender—it's worse if you
    fights or you runs:
  You may hide in the caves, they'll be only your graves,
    but you can't get away from the guns!

You may talk o' gin and beer
  When you're quartered safe out 'ere,
An' you're sent to penny-fights an' Aldershot it;
But when it comes to slaughter
You will do your work on water,
An' you'll lick the bloomin' boots of 'im that's got it.
Now in Injia's sunny clime,
Where I used to spend my time
A-servin' of 'Er Majesty the Queen,
Of all them blackfaced crew
The finest man I knew
Was our regimental bhisti, Gunga Din,
        He was 'Din! Din! Din!
  'You limpin' lump o' brick-dust, Gunga Din!
        'Hi! Slippy *hitherao*!
        'Water, get it! *Panee lao*,[1]
  'You squidgy-nosed old idol, Gunga Din.'

The uniform 'e wore
Was nothin' much before,
An' rather less than 'arf o' that be'ind,
For a piece o' twisty rag
An' a goatskin water-bag
Was all the field-equipment 'e could find.
When the sweatin' troop-train lay
In a sidin' through the day,
Where the 'eat would make your bloomin' eyebrows
        crawl,
We shouted 'Harry By!'[2]
Till our throats were bricky-dry,
Then we wopped 'im 'cause 'e couldn't serve us all.

[1] Bring water swiftly.
[2] O brother.

It was 'Din! Din! Din!
'You 'eathen, where the mischief 'ave you been?
    'You put some *juldee*[1] in it
    'Or I'll *marrow*[2] you this minute
'If you don't fill up my helmet, Gunga Din!'

'E would dot an' carry one
Till the longest day was done;
An' 'e didn't seem to know the use o' fear.
If we charged or broke or cut,
You could bet your bloomin' nut,
'E'd be waitin' fifty paces right flank rear.
With 'is mussick[3] on 'is back,
'E would skip with our attack,
An' watch us till the bugles made 'Retire,'
An' for all 'is dirty 'ide
'E was white, clear white, inside
When 'e went to tend the wounded under fire!
    It was 'Din! Din! Din!'
With the bullets kickin' dust-spots on the green.
    When the cartridges ran out,
    You could hear the front-ranks shout,
'Hi! ammunition-mules an' Gunga Din!'

I shan't forgit the night
When I dropped be'ind the fight
With a bullet where my belt-plate should 'a' been.
I was chokin' mad with thirst,
An' the man that spied me first
Was our good old grinnin', gruntin' Gunga Din.
'E lifted up my 'ead,
An' he plugged me where I bled,
An' 'e guv me 'arf-a-pint o' water green.

[1] Be quick.
[2] Hit you.
[3] Water-skin.

It was crawlin' and it stunk.
But of all the drinks I've drunk,
I'm gratefullest to one from Gunga Din.
     It was 'Din! Din! Din!
  ''Ere's a beggar with a bullet through 'is spleen;
    ''E's chawin' up the ground,
    'An' 'e's kickin' all around:
  'For Gawd's sake git the water, Gunga Din!'

'E carried me away
To where a dooli lay,
An' a bullet come an' drilled the beggar clean.
'E put me safe inside,
An' just before 'e died,
'I 'ope you liked your drink,' sez Gunga Din.
So I'll meet 'im later on
At the place where 'e is gone—
Where it's always double drill and no canteen.
'E'll be squattin' on the coals
Givin' drink to poor damned souls,
An' I'll get a swig in hell from Gunga Din!
     Yes, Din! Din! Din!
  You Lazarushian-leather Gunga Din!
    Though I've belted you and flayed you,
    By the livin' Gawd that made you,
  You're a better man than I am, Gunga Din!

THE WIDOW AT WINDSOR

'Ave you 'eard o' the Widow at Windsor
  With a hairy gold crown on 'er 'ead?
She 'as ships on the foam—she 'as millions at 'ome
  An' she pays us poor beggars in red.
    (Ow, poor beggars in red!)

There's 'er nick on the cavalry 'orses,
   There's 'er mark on the medical stores—
An' 'er troopers you'll find with a fair wind be'ind
   That takes us to various wars.
      (Poor beggars!—barbarious wars!)
         Then 'ere's to the Widow at Windsor,
            An' 'ere's to the stores an' the guns,
         The men an' the 'orses what makes up the forces
            O' Missis Victorier's sons.
      (Poor beggars! Victorier's sons!)

Walk wide o' the Widow at Windsor,
   For 'alf o' Creation she owns:
We 'ave bought 'er the same with the sword an' the flame,
   An' we've salted it down with our bones.
      (Poor beggars!—it's blue with our bones!)
Hands off o' the sons o' the Widow,
   Hands off o' the goods in 'er shop,
For the Kings must come down an' the Emperors frown
   When the Widow at Windsor says 'Stop!'
      (Poor beggars!—we're sent to say 'Stop!')
         Then 'ere's to the Lodge o' the Widow,
            From the Pole to the Tropics it runs—
         To the Lodge that we tile with the rank an' the
            file,
            An' open in form with the guns.
      (Poor beggars!—it's always they guns!)

We 'ave 'eard o' the Widow at Windsor,
   It's safest to leave 'er alone:
For 'er sentries we stand by the sea an' the land
   Wherever the bugles are blown.
      (Poor beggars!—an' don't we get blown!)
Take 'old o' the Wings o' the Mornin',
   An' flop round the earth till you're dead;

But you won't get away from the tune that they play
    To the bloomin' old rag over'ead.
        (Poor beggars!—it's 'ot over'ead!)
            Then 'ere's to the Sons o' the Widow,
                Wherever, 'owever they roam.
            'Ere's all they desire, an' if they require
                A speedy return to their 'ome.
            (Poor beggars!—they'll never see 'ome!)

BELTS

There was a row in Silver Street that's near to Dublin
    Quay,
Between an Irish regiment an' English cavalree;
It started at Revelly an' it lasted on till dark:
The first man dropped at Harrison's, the last forninst the
    Park.
            For it was:—'Belts, belts, belts, an' that's one for
                you!'
            An' it was 'Belts, belts, belts, an' that's done for
                you!'
            O buckle an' tongue
            Was the song that we sung
            From Harrison's down to the Park!

There was a row in Silver Street—the regiments was
    out,
They called us 'Delhi Rebels,' an' we answered 'Threes
    about!'
That drew them like a hornets' nest—we met them good
    an' large,
The English at the double an' the Irish at the charge.
            Then it was:—'Belts, etc.'

183

There was a row in Silver Street—an' I was in it too;
We passed the time o' day, an' then the belts went whir-
    raru!
I misremember what occurred, but, subsequint the storm,
A *Freeman's Journal Supplemint* was all *my* uniform.
        O it was:—'Belts, etc.'

There was a row in Silver Street—they sent the Polis there,
The English were too drunk to know, the Irish didn't
    care;
But when they grew impertinint we simultaneous rose,
Till half o' them was Liffey mud an' half was tatthered
    clo'es.
        For it was:—'Belts, etc.'

There was a row in Silver Street—it might ha' raged till
    now,
But some one drew his side-arm clear, an' nobody knew
    how;
'Twas Hogan took the point an' dropped; we saw the red
    blood run:
An' so we all was murderers that started out in fun.
        While it was:—'Belts, etc.'

There was a row in Silver Street—but that put down the
    shine,
Wid each man whisperin' to his next:—''Twas never work
    o' mine!'
We went away like beaten dogs, an' down the street we
    bore him,
The poor dumb corpse that couldn't tell the bhoys were
    sorry for him.
        When it was:—'Belts, etc.'

There was a row in Silver Street—it isn't over yet,
For half of us are under guard wid punishments to get;

'Tis all a merricle to me as in the Clink I lie:
There was a row in Silver Street—begod, I wonder
why!
But it was:—'Belts, belts, belts, an' that's one for
you!'
An' it was, 'Belts, belts, belts, an' that's done for
you!'
O buckle an' tongue
Was the song that we sung
From Harrison's down to the Park!

THE YOUNG BRITISH SOLDIER

When the 'arf-made recruity goes out to the East
'E acts like a babe an' 'e drinks like a beast,
An' 'e wonders because 'e is frequent deceased
Ere 'e's fit for to serve as a soldier.
Serve, serve, serve as a soldier,
Serve, serve, serve as a soldier
Serve, serve, serve as a soldier,
So-oldier *of* the Queen!

Now all you recruities what's drafted to-day,
You shut up your rag-box an' 'ark to my lay,
An' I'll sing you a soldier as far as I may:
A soldier what's fit for a soldier.
Fit, fit, fit for a soldier . . .

First mind you steer clear o' the grog-sellers' huts,
For they sell you Fixed Bay'nets that rots out your
guts—
Ay, drink that 'ud eat the live steel from your butts—
An' it's bad for the young British soldier.
Bad, bad, bad for the soldier . . .

When the cholera comes—as it will past a doubt—
Keep out of the wet and don't go on the shout,
For the sickness gets in as the liquor dies out,
    An' it crumples the young British soldier.
        Crum-, crum-, crumples the soldier . . .

But the worst o' your foes is the sun over'ead:
You *must* wear your 'elmet for all that is said:
If 'e finds you uncovered 'e'll knock you down dead,
    An' you'll die like a fool of a soldier.
        Fool, fool, fool of a soldier . . .

If you're cast for fatigue by a sergeant unkind,
Don't grouse like a woman nor crack on nor blind;
Be handy and civil, and then you will find
    That it's beer for the young British soldier.
        Beer, beer, beer for the soldier . . .

Now, if you must marry, take care she is old—
A troop-sergeant's widow's the nicest, I'm told,
For beauty won't help if your rations is cold,
    Nor love ain't enough for a soldier.
        'Nough, 'nough, 'nough for a soldier . . .

If the wife should go wrong with a comrade, be loth
To shoot when you catch 'em—you'll swing, on my
      oath!—
Make 'im take 'er and keep 'er: that's Hell for them
      both,
    An' you're shut o' the curse of a soldier.
        Curse, curse, curse of a soldier . . .

When first under fire an' you're wishful to duck
Don't look nor take 'eed at the man that is struck.
Be thankful you're livin', and trust to your luck
    And march to your front like a soldier.
        Front, front, front like a soldier . . .

When 'arf of your bullets fly wide in the ditch,
Don't call your Martini a cross-eyed old bitch;
She's human as you are—you treat her as sich,
    An' she'll fight for the young British soldier
        Fight, fight, fight for the soldier . . .

When shakin' their bustles like ladies so fine,
The guns o' the enemy wheel into line,
Shoot low at the limbers an' don't mind the shine,
    For noise never startles the soldier.
        Start-, start-, startles the soldier . . .

If your officer's dead and the sergeants look white,
Remember it's ruin to run from a fight:
So take open order, lie down, and sit tight,
    And wait for supports like a soldier.
        Wait, wait, wait like a soldier . . .

When you're wounded and left on Afghanistan's plains,
And the women come out to cut up what remains,
Jest roll to your rifle and blow out your brains
    An' go to your Gawd like a soldier.
      Go, go, go like a soldier,
      Go, go, go like a soldier,
      Go, go, go like a soldier,
        So-oldier *of* the Queen!

MANDALAY

By the old Moulmein Pagoda, lookin' lazy at the sea,
  There's a Burma girl a-settin', and I know she thinks
    o' me;
For the wind is in the palm-trees, and the temple-bells they
    say:
'Come you back, you British soldier; come you back to
    Mandalay!'

Come you back to Mandalay,
Where the old Flotilla lay:
Can't you 'ear their paddles chunkin' from Ran-
goon to Mandalay?
On the road to Mandalay,
Where the flyin'-fishes play,
An' the dawn comes up like thunder outer China
'crost the Bay!

'Er petticoat was yaller an' 'er little cap was green,
An' 'er name was Supi-yaw-lat—jes' the same as Thee-
baw's Queen,
An' I seed her first a-smokin' of a whackin' white cheroot,
An' a-wastin' Christian kisses on an 'eathen idol's
foot:
Bloomin' idol made o' mud—
Wot they called the Great Gawd Budd—
Plucky lot she cared for idols when I kissed 'er
where she stud!
On the road to Mandalay . . .

When the mist was on the rice-fields an' the sun was
droppin' slow,
She'd git 'er little banjo an' she'd sing ' *Kulla-lo-lo!* '
With 'er arm upon my shoulder an' 'er cheek agin my
cheek
We useter watch the steamers an' the *hathis* pilin' teak.
Elephints a-pilin' teak
In the sludgy, squdgy creek,
Where the silence 'ung that 'eavy you was 'arf
afraid to speak!
On the road to Mandalay . . .

But that's all shove be'ind me—long ago an' fur away,
An' there ain't no 'buses runnin' from the Bank to Man-
dalay;

An' I'm learnin' 'ere in London what the ten-year soldier
    tells:
'If you've 'eard the East a-callin', you won't never 'eed
    naught else.'
        No! you won't 'eed nothin' else
        But them spicy garlic smells,
        An' the sunshine an' the' palm-trees an' the
          tinkly temple-bells;
        On the road to Mandalay . . .

I am sick o' wastin' leather on these gritty pavin'-stones,
An' the blasted English drizzle wakes the fever in my
    bones;
Tho' I walks with fifty 'ousemaids outer Chelsea to the
    Strand,
An' they talks a lot o' lovin', but wot do they understand?
        Beefy face an' grubby 'and—
        Law! wot do they understand?
        I've a neater, sweeter maiden in a cleaner, greener
          land!
        On the road to Mandalay . . .

Ship me somewheres east of Suez, where the best is like
    the worst,
Where there aren't no Ten Commandments an' a man can
    raise a thirst;
For the temple-bells are callin', an' it's there that I would
    be—
By the old Moulmein Pagoda, looking lazy at the sea;
        On the road to Mandalay.
        Where the old Flotilla lay,
        With our sick beneath the awnings when we went
          to Mandalay!
        On the road to Mandalay,
        Where the flyin'-fishes play,
        An' the dawn comes up like thunder outer China
          'crost the Bay!

TROOPIN'

(*Old English Army in the East*)

Troopin', troopin', troopin' to the sea:
    'Ere's September come again—the six-year men are
        free.
O leave the dead be'ind us, for they cannot come away
To where the ship's a-coalin' up that takes us 'ome
        to-day.
            We're goin' 'ome, we're goin' 'ome,
                Our ship is *at* the shore,
            An' you must pack your 'aversack,
                For we won't come back no more.
            Ho, don't you grieve for me,
                My lovely Mary-Ann!
            For I'll marry you yit on a fourp'ny bit
                As a time-expired man.

The *Malabar's* in 'arbour with the *Jumner* at 'er tail,
An' the time-expired's waitin' of 'is orders for to sail.
Ho! the weary waitin' when on Khyber 'ills we lay,
But the time-expired's waitin' of 'is orders 'ome to-day.

They'll turn us out at Portsmouth wharf in cold an' wet an'
        rain,
All wearin' Injian cotton kit, but we will not complain,
They'll kill us of pneumonia—for that's their little way—
But damn the chills and fever, men, we're goin' 'ome
        to-day!

Troopin', troopin', winter's round again!
See the new draf's pourin' in for the old campaign;
Ho, you poor recruities, but you've got to earn your pay—
What's the last from Lunnon, lads? We're goin' there
        to-day.

Troopin', troopin', give another cheer—
'Ere's to English women an' a quart of English beer.
The Colonel an' the Regiment an' all who've got to stay,
Gawd's Mercy strike 'em gentle! Whoop! we're goin'
    'ome to-day.
        We're goin' 'ome, we're goin' 'ome,
          Our ship is *at* the shore,
        An' you must pack your 'aversack,
          For we won't come back no more.
        Ho, don't you grieve for me,
          My lovely Mary-Ann!
        For I'll marry you yit on a fourp'ny bit
          As a time-expired man.

THE WIDOW'S PARTY

'Where have you been this while away,
        Johnnie, Johnnie?'
Out with the rest on a picnic lay,
        Johnnie, my Johnnie, aha!
They called us out of the barrack-yard
To Gawd knows where from Gosport Hard,
And you can't refuse when you get the card,
        And the Widow gives the party.
          (*Bugle*: Ta—rara—ra-ra-rara!)

'What did you get to eat and drink,
        Johnnie, Johnnie?'
Standing water as thick as ink,
        Johnnie, my Johnnie, aha!
A bit o' beef that were three year stored,
A bit of mutton as tough as a board,
And a fowl we killed with a sergeant's sword,
        When the Widow give the party.

'What did you do for knives and forks,
         Johnnie, Johnnie?'
We carries 'em with us wherever we walks,
         Johnnie, my Johnnie, aha!
And some was sliced and some was halved,
And some was crimped and some was carved,
And some was gutted and some was starved,
         When the Widow give the party.

'What ha' you done with half your mess,
         Johnnie, Johnnie?'
They couldn't do more and they wouldn't do less,
         Johnnie, my Johnnie, aha!
They ate their whack and they drank their fill,
And I think the rations has made them ill,
For half my comp'ny's lying still
         Where the Widow give the party.

'How did you get away—away,
         Johnnie, Johnnie?'
On the broad o' my back at the end o' the day,
         Johnnie, my Johnnie, aha!
I comed away like a bleedin' toff,
For I got four niggers to carry me off,
As I lay in the bight of a canvas trough,
         When the Widow give the party.

'What was the end of all the show,
         Johnnie, Johnnie?'
Ask my Colonel, for I don't know,
         Johnnie, my Johnnie, aha!
We broke a King and we built a road—
A court-house stands where the Reg'ment goed.
And the river's clean where the raw blood flowed
         When the Widow give the party.
             (*Bugle*: Ta—rara—ra-ra-rara!)

GENTLEMEN-RANKERS

To the legion of the lost ones, to the cohort of the
    damned,
  To my brethren in their sorrow overseas,
Sings a gentleman of England cleanly bred, machinely
    crammed,
  And a trooper of the Empress, if you please.
Yes, a trooper of the forces who has run his own six
    horses,
  And faith he went the pace and went it blind,
And the world was more than kin while he held the ready
    tin,
  But to-day the Sergeant's something less than kind.
      We're poor little lambs who've lost our way,
        Baa! Baa! Baa!
      We're little black sheep who've gone astray,
        Baa—aa—aa!
      Gentlemen-rankers out on the spree,
      Damned from here to Eternity,
      God ha' mercy on such as we,
        Baa! Yah! Bah!

Oh, it's sweet to sweat through stables, sweet to empty
    kitchen slops,
  And it's sweet to hear the tales the troopers tell,
To dance with blowzy housemaids at the regimental
    hops
  And thrash the cad who says you waltz too well.
Yes, it makes you cock-a-hoop to be 'Rider' to your
    troop,
  And branded with a blasted worsted spur,
When you envy, O how keenly, one poor Tommy living
    cleanly
  Who blacks your boots and sometimes calls you
    'Sir.'

If the home we never write to, and the oaths we never keep,
 And all we know most distant and most dear,
Across the snoring barrack-room return to break our sleep,
 Can you blame us if we soak ourselves in beer?
When the drunken comrade mutters and the great guard-
 lantern gutters
 And the horror of our fall is written plain,
Every secret, self-revealing on the aching whitewashed
 ceiling,
 Do you wonder that we drug ourselves from pain?

We have done with Hope and Honour, we are lost to Love
 and Truth,
 We are dropping down the ladder rung by rung,
And the measure of our torment is the measure of our
 youth.
 God help us, for we knew the worst too young!
Our shame is clean repentance for the crime that brought
 the sentence,
 Our pride it is to know no spur of pride,
And the Curse of Reuben holds us till an alien turf enfolds
 us
 And we die, and none can tell Them where we died.
    We're poor little lambs who've lost our way,
      Baa! Baa! Baa!
    We're little black sheep who've gone astray,
      Baa—aa—aa!
    Gentlemen-rankers out on the spree,
    Damned from here to Eternity,
    God ha' mercy on such as we,
      Baa! Yah! Bah!

194

PRIVATE ORTHERIS'S SONG

('The Courting of Dinah Shadd'—*Life's Handicap*)

My girl she give me the go onest,
    When I was a London lad;
An' I went on the drink for a fortnight,
    An' then I went to the bad.
The Queen she give me a shillin'
    To fight for 'er over the seas;
But Guv'ment built me a fever-trap,
    An' Injia give me disease.
(*Chorus*) Ho! don't you 'eed what a girl says,
            An' don't you go for the beer;
        But I was an ass when I was at grass,
            An' that is why I'm 'ere.

I fired a shot at a Afghan,
    The beggar 'e fired again,
An' I lay on my bed with a 'ole in my 'ed,
    An' missed the next campaign!
I up with my gun at a Burman
    Who carried a bloomin' *dah*,
But the cartridge stuck and the bay'nit bruk,
    An' all I got was the scar.
(*Chorus*) Ho! don't you aim at a Afghan,
            When you stand on the skyline clear;
        An' don't you go for a Burman
            If none o' your friends is near.

I served my time for a Corp'ral,
    An' wetted my stripes with pop,
For I went on the bend with a intimate friend,
    An' finished the night in the 'shop.'

I served my time for a Sergeant;
  The Colonel 'e sez 'No!
The most you'll see is a full C.B.'
  An' . . . very next night 'twas so!
(*Chorus*) Ho! don't you go for a Corp'ral
          Unless your 'ed is clear;
        But I was an ass when I was at grass,
          An' that is why I'm 'ere.

I've tasted the luck o' the Army
  In barrack an' camp an' clink.
An' I lost my tip through the bloomin' trip
  Along o' the women an' drink.
I'm down at the heel o' my service,
  An' when I am laid on the shelf,
My very worst friend from beginning to end
  By the blood of a mouse was myself!
(*Chorus*) Ho! don't you 'eed what a girl says,
          An' don't you go for the beer;
        But I was an ass when I was at grass,
          An' that is why I'm 'ere!

SHILLIN' A DAY

My name is O'Kelly, I've heard the Revelly
  From Birr to Bareilly, from Leeds to Lahore,
Hong-Kong and Peshawur,
Lucknow and Etawah,
And fifty-five more all endin' in 'pore'.
Black Death and his quickness, the depth and the thickness
Of sorrow and sickness I've known on my way,
But I'm old and I'm nervis,
I'm cast from the Service,
And all I deserve is a shillin' a day.

196

(*Chorus*)   Shillin' a day,
            Bloomin' good pay—
            Lucky to touch it, a shillin' a day!

Oh, it drives me half crazy to think of the days I
Went slap for the Ghazi, my sword at my side,
When we rode Hell-for-leather
Both squadrons together,
That didn't care whether we lived or we died.
But it's no use despairin', my wife must go charin'
An' me commissairin', the pay-bills to better,
So if me you be'old
In the wet and the cold,
By the Grand Metropold, won't you give me a letter?

(*Full chorus*)   Give 'im a letter—
            'Can't do no better,
            Late Troop-Sergeant-Major an'—runs with
              a letter!
            Think what 'e's been,
            Think what 'e's seen.
            Think of his pension an'——
            GAWD SAVE THE QUEEN!

'BACK TO THE ARMY AGAIN'

I'm 'ere in a ticky ulster an' a broken billycock 'at,
A-layin' on to the sergeant I don't know a gun from a
    bat;
My shirt's doin' duty for jacket, my sock's stickin' out o'
    my boots,
An' I'm learnin' the damned old goose-step along o' the
    new recruits!

197

Back to the Army again, sergeant,
   Back to the Army again.
Don't look so 'ard, for I 'aven't no card,
   I'm back to the Army again!

I done my six years' service. 'Er Majesty sez: 'Good day—
You'll please to come when you're rung for, an' 'ere's your
     'ole back-pay;
An' fourpence a day for baccy—an' bloomin' gen'rous,
     too;
An' now you can make your fortune—the same as your
     orf'cers do.'

   Back to the Army again, sergeant,
      Back to the Army again.
   'Ow did I learn to do right-about-turn?
      I'm back to the Army again!

A man o' four-an'-twenty that 'asn't learned of a trade—
Beside 'Reserve' agin' him—'e'd better be never made.
I tried my luck for a quarter, an' that was enough for me,
An' I thought of 'Er Majesty's barricks, an' I thought I'd
     go an' see.

   Back to the Army again, sergeant,
      Back to the Army again.
   'Tisn't my fault if I dress when I 'alt—
      I'm back to the Army again!

The sergeant arst no questions, but 'e winked the other eye,
'E sez to me, "'Shun!' an' I shunted, the same as in days
     gone by;
For 'e saw the set o' my shoulders, an' I couldn't 'elp
     'oldin' straight
When me an' the other rookies come under the barrick-
     gate.

Back to the Army again, sergeant,
    Back to the Army again.
'Oo would ha' thought I could carry an' port?[1]
    I'm back to the Army again!

I took my bath, an' I wallered—for, Gawd, I needed it so!
I smelt the smell o' the barricks, I 'eard the bugles go.
I 'eard the feet on the gravel—the feet o' the men what
    drill—
An' I sez to my flutterin' 'eart-strings, I sez to 'em, 'Peace,
    be still!'

Back to the Army again, sergeant,
    Back to the Army again.
'Oo said I knew when the troopship was due?
    I'm back to the Army again!

I carried my slops to the tailor; I sez to 'im, 'None o' your
    lip!
You tight 'em over the shoulders, an' loose 'em over the
    'ip,
For the set o' the tunic's 'orrid.' An' 'e sez to me, 'Strike
    me dead,
But I thought you was used to the business!' an' so 'e done
    what I said.

Back to the Army again, sergeant,
    Back to the Army again.
Rather too free with my fancies? Wot—me?
    I'm back to the Army again!

Next week I'll 'ave 'em fitted; I'll buy me a swagger-
    cane;
They'll let me free o' the barricks to walk on the Hoe
    again,

[1] Carry and port his rifle.

199

In the name o' William Parsons, that used to be Edward
    Clay,
An'—any pore beggar that wants it can draw my fourpence
    a day!

      Back to the Army again, sergeant,
        Back to the Army again.
      Out o' the cold an' the rain, sergeant,
        Out o' the cold an' the rain.
                'Oo's there?

      A man that's too good to be lost you,
        A man that is 'andled an' made—
      A man that will pay what 'e cost you
        In learnin' the others their trade—parade!
      You're droppin' the pick o' the Army
        Because you don't 'elp 'em remain,
      But drives 'em to cheat to get out o' the street
        An' back to the Army again!

'BIRDS OF PREY' MARCH

(*Troops for Foreign Service*)

March! The mud is cakin' good about our trousies.
  Front!—eyes front, an' watch the Colour-casin's
  drip.
Front! The faces of the women in the 'ouses
  Ain't the kind o' things to take aboard the ship.

Cheer! An' we'll never march to victory.
Cheer! An' we'll never live to 'ear the cannon roar!
    The Large Birds o' Prey
    They will carry us away,
An' you'll never see your soldiers any more!

Wheel! Oh, keep your touch; we're goin' round a
     corner.
  Time!—mark time, an' let the men be'ind us close.
Lord! The transport's full, an' 'alf our lot not on 'er—
  Cheer, Oh, cheer! We're going off where no one
     knows.

March! The Devil's none so black as 'e is painted!
  Cheer! We'll 'ave some fun before we're put away.
'Alt an' 'and 'er out—a woman's gone and fainted!
  Cheer! Get on!—Gawd 'elp the married men to-day!

Hoi! Come up, you 'ungry beggars, to yer sorrow.
  ('Ear them say they want their tea, an' want it quick!)
You won't have no mind for slingers,[1] not to-morrow—
  No; you'll put the 'tween-decks stove out, bein' sick!

'Alt! The married kit 'as all to go before us!
  'Course it's blocked the bloomin' gangway up again!
Cheer, Oh, cheer the 'Orse Guards watchin' tender
     o'er us,
  Keepin' us since eight this mornin' in the rain!

Stuck in 'eavy marchin'-order, sopped and wringin'—
  Sick, before our time to watch 'er 'eave an' fall,
'Ere's your 'appy 'ome at last, an' stop your singin'.
  'Alt! Fall in along the troop-deck! Silence all!

Cheer! For we'll never live to see no bloomin' victory!
Cheer! An' we'll never live to 'ear the cannon roar!
          (One cheer more!)
             The jackal an' the kite
              'Ave an 'ealthy appetite,
An' you'll never see your soldiers any more! ('Ip! Urroar!)

[1] Bread soaked in tea.

201

The eagle an' the crow
They are waitin' ever so,
An' you'll never see your soldiers any more! ('Ip! Urroar!)
Yes, the Large Birds o' Prey
They will carry us away,
An' you'll never see your soldiers any more!

'SOLDIER AN' SAILOR TOO'

(*The Royal Regiment of Marines*)

As I was spittin' into the Ditch aboard o' the *Crocodile*,
I seed a man on a man-o'-war got up in the Reg'lars
style.
'E was scrapin' the paint from off of 'er plates, an' I sez to
'im, "'Oo are you?'
Sez 'e, 'I'm a Jolly—'Er Majesty's Jolly—soldier an' sailor
too!'
Now 'is work begins by Gawd knows when, and 'is work
is never through;
'E isn't one o' the reg'lar Line, nor 'e isn't one of the crew.
'E's a kind of a giddy harumfrodite—soldier an' sailor too!

An', after, I met 'im all over the world, a-doin' all kinds of
things,
Like landin' 'isself with a Gatlin' gun to talk to them
'eathen kings;
'E sleeps in an 'ammick instead of a cot, an' 'e drills with
the deck on a slew,
An' 'e sweats like a Jolly—'Er Majesty's Jolly—soldier
an' sailor too!
For there isn't a job on the top o' the earth the beggar don't
know, nor do—

202

You can leave 'im at night cn a bald man's 'ead, to paddle
'is own canoe—
'E's a sort of a bloomin' cosmopolouse—soldier an' sailor
too.

We've fought 'em in trooper, we've fought 'em in dock,
and drunk with 'em in betweens,
When they called us the seasick scull'ry-maids, an' we
called 'em the Ass-Marines;
But, when we was down for a double fatigue, from Wool-
wich to Bernardmyo,
We sent for the Jollies—'Er Majesty's Jollies—soldier an'
sailor too!
They think for 'emselves, an' they steal for 'emselves, and
they never ask what's to do,
But they're camped an' fed an' they're up an' fed before
our bugle's blew.
Ho! they ain't no limpin' procrastitutes—soldier an'
sailor too.

You may say we are fond of an 'arness-cut, or 'ootin' in
barrick-yards,
Or startin' a Board School mutiny along o' the Onion
Guards;[1]
But once in a while we can finish in style for the ends of the
earth to view,
The same as the Jollies—'Er Majesty's Jollies—soldier an'
sailor too!
They come of our lot, they was brothers to us; they was
beggars we'd met an' knew;
Yes, barrin' an inch in the chest an' the arm, they was
doubles o' me an' you;
For they weren't no special chrysanthemums—soldier an'
sailor too!

[1] Long ago, a battalion of the Guards was sent to Bermuda as a punish-
ment for riotous conduct in barracks.

To take your chance in the thick of a rush, with firing all
about,
Is nothing so bad when you've cover to 'and, an' leave an'
likin' to shout;
But to stand an' be still to the *Birken'ead* drill[1] is a damn'
tough bullet to chew,
An' they done it, the Jollies—'Er Majesty's Jollies—
soldier an' sailor too!
Their work was done when it 'adn't begun; they was
younger nor me an' you;
Their choice it was plain between drownin' in 'eaps an'
bein' mopped by the screw,
So they stood an' was still to the *Birken'ead* drill, soldier
an' sailor too!

We're most of us liars, we're 'arf of us thieves, an' the rest
are as rank as can be,
But once in a while we can finish in style (which I 'ope it
won't 'appen to me).
But it makes you think better o' you an' your friends, an'
the work you may 'ave to do,
When you think o' the sinkin' *Victorier's*[2] Jollies—soldier
an' sailor too!
Now there isn't no room for to say ye don't know—they
'ave proved it plain and true—
That, whether it's Widow, or whether's it's ship, Victorier's
work is to do,
An' they done it, the Jollies—'Er Majesty's Jollies—soldier
an' sailor too!

[1] In 1852 the *Birkenhead* transport was sunk off Simon's Bay. The
Marines aboard her went down as drawn up on her deck.
[2] Admiral Tryon's flagship, sunk in collision in 1893.

SAPPERS

(*Royal Engineers*)

When the Waters were dried an' the Earth did appear,
    ('It's all one,' says the Sapper),
The Lord He created the Engineer,
  Her Majesty's Royal Engineer,
  With the rank and pay of a Sapper!

When the Flood come along for an extra monsoon,
'Twas Noah constructed the first pontoon
  To the plans of Her Majesty's, etc.

But after fatigue in the wet an' the sun,
Old Noah got drunk, which he wouldn't ha' done
  If he'd trained with, etc.

When the Tower o' Babel had mixed up men's *bat*,[1]
Some clever civilian was managing that,
  An' none of, etc.

When the Jews had a fight at the foot of a hill,
Young Joshua ordered the sun to stand still,
  For he was a Captain of Engineers, etc.

When the Children of Israel made bricks without straw,
They were learnin' the regular work of our Corps,
  The work of, etc.

For ever since then, if a war they would wage,
Behold us a-shinin' on history's page—
  First page for, etc.

[1] Talk.

We lay down their sidings an' help 'em entrain,
An' we sweep up their mess through the bloomin' cam-
   paign,
   In the style of, etc.

They send us in front with a fuse an' a mine
To blow up the gates that are rushed by the Line,
   But bent by, etc.

They send us behind with a pick an' a spade,
To dig for the guns of a bullock-brigade
   Which has asked for, etc.

We work under escort in trousers and shirt,
An' the heathen they plug us tail-up in the dirt,
   Annoying, etc.

We blast out the rock an' we shovel the mud,
We make 'em good roads an'—they roll down the *khud*[1]
   Reporting, etc.

We make 'em their bridges, their wells, an' their huts,
An' the telegraph-wire the enemy cuts,
   An' it's blamed on, etc.

An' when we return, an' from war we would cease,
They grudge us adornin' the billets of peace,
   Which are kept for, etc.

We build 'em nice barracks—they swear they are bad,
That our Colonels are Methodist, married or mad,
   Insultin', etc.

They haven't no manners nor gratitude too,
For the more that we help 'em, the less will they do,
   But mock at, etc.

[1] Hillside.

Now the Line's but a man with a gun in his hand,
An' Cavalry's only what horses can stand,
    When helped by, etc.

Artillery moves by the leave o' the ground,
But *we* are the men that do something all round.
    For *we* are, etc.

I have stated it plain, an' my argument's thus
    ('It's all one,' says the Sapper)
There's only one Corps which is perfect—that's us;
    An' they call us Her Majesty's Engineers,
    Her Majesty's Royal Engineers,
    With the rank and pay of a Sapper!

THAT DAY

It got beyond all orders an' it got beyond all 'ope;
    It got to shammin' wounded an' retirin' from the 'alt.
'Ole companies was lookin' for the nearest road to slope;
    It were just a bloomin' knock-out—an' our fault!

> *Now there ain't no chorus 'ere to give,*
>   *Nor there ain't no band to play;*
> *An' I wish I was dead 'fore I done what I did,*
>   *Or seen what I seed that day!*

We was sick o' bein' punished, an' we let 'em know it, too;
    An' a company-commander up an' 'it us with a sword,
An' someone shouted. ''Ook it!' an' it come to *sove-ki-poo*,
    An' we chucked our rifles from us—O my Gawd!

There was thirty dead an' wounded on the ground we
    wouldn't keep—
    No, there wasn't more than twenty when the front begun
      to go—
But, Christ! along the line o' flight they cut us up like
    sheep,
    An' that was all we gained by doin' so!

I 'eard the knives be'ind me, but I dursn't face my man,
    Nor I don't know where I went to, 'cause I didn't 'alt to
      see,
Till I 'eard a beggar squealin' out for quarter as 'e ran,
    An' I thought I knew the voice an'—it was me!

We was 'idin' under bedsteads more than 'arf a march
      away:
    We was lyin' up like rabbits all about the country-side;
An' the Major cursed 'is Maker 'cause 'e'd lived to see
      that day,
    An' the Colonel broke 'is sword acrost, an' cried.

We was rotten 'fore we started—we was never disciplined;
    We made it out a favour if an order was obeyed.
Yes, every little drummer 'ad 'is rights an' wrongs to mind,
    So we had to pay for teachin'—an' we paid!

The papers 'id it 'andsome, but you know the Army knows;
    We was put to groomin' camels till the regiments with-
      drew,
An' they gave us each a medal for subduin' England's foes,
    An' I 'ope you like my song—because it's true!

> *An' there ain't no chorus 'ere to give,*
>   *Nor there ain't no band to play;*
> *But I wish I was dead 'fore I done what I did,*
>   *Or seen what I seed that day!*

'THE MEN THAT FOUGHT AT MINDEN'

(*In the Lodge of Instruction*)

The men that fought at Minden, they was rookies in
their time—
So was them that fought at Waterloo!
All the 'ole command, yuss, from Minden to Maiwand,
They was once dam' sweeps like you!

Then do not be discouraged, 'Eaven is your 'elper,
We'll learn you not to forget;
An' you mustn't swear an' curse, or you'll only catch it
worse,
For we'll make you soldiers yet!

The men that fought at Minden, they 'ad stocks beneath
their chins,
Six inch 'igh an' more;
But fatigue it was their pride, and they *would* not be
denied
To clean the cook-'ouse floor.

The men that fought at Minden, they had anarchistic
bombs
Served to 'em by name of 'and-grenades;
But they got it in the eye (same as you will by-an'-by)
When they clubbed their field-parades.

The men that fought at Minden, they 'ad buttons up an'
down,
Two-an'-twenty dozen of 'em told;
But they didn't grouse an' shirk at an hour's extry
work,
They kept 'em bright as gold.

The men that fought at Minden, they was armed with
    musketoons,
    Also, they was drilled by 'alberdiers.
I don't know what they were, but the sergeants took good
    care
    They washed be'ind their ears.

The men that fought at Minden, they 'ad ever cash in 'and
    Which they did not bank nor save,
But spent it gay an' free on their betters—such as me—
    For the good advice I gave.

The men that fought at Minden, they was civil—yuss, they
    was—
    Never didn't talk o' rights an' wrongs,
But they got it with the toe (same as you will get it—so!)—
    For interrupting songs.

The men that fought at Minden, they was several other
    things
    Which I don't remember clear;
But *that's* the reason why, now the six-year men are dry,
    The rooks will stand the beer!

Then do not be discouraged, 'Eaven is your 'elper,
    We'll learn you not to forget.
An' you mustn't swear an' curse, or you'll only catch it
    worse,
    An' we'll make you soldiers yet!

Soldiers yet, if you've got it in you—
    All for the sake of the Core;
Soldiers yet, if we 'ave to skin you—
    Run an' get the beer, Johnny Raw—Johnny Raw!
    Ho! run an' get the beer, Johnny Raw!

I've taken my fun where I've found it;
I've rogued an' I've ranged in my time
I've 'ad my pickin' o' sweethearts,
   An' four o' the lot was prime.
One was an 'arf-caste widow,
   One was a woman at Prome,
One was the wife of a *jemadar-sais*,[1]
   An' one is a girl at 'ome.

Now I aren't no 'and with the ladies,
   For, takin' 'em all along,
You never can say till you've tried 'em,
   An' then you are like to be wrong.
There's times when you'll think that you mightn't,
   There's times when you'll know that you might;
But the things you will learn from the Yellow an' Brown,
   They'll 'elp you a lot with the White!

I was a young un at 'Oogli,
   Shy as a girl to begin;
Aggie de Castrer she made me,
   An' Aggie was clever as sin;
Older than me, but my first un—
   More like a mother she were—
Showed me the way to promotion an' pay,
   An' I learned about women from 'er!

Then I was ordered to Burma,
   Actin' in charge o' Bazar,
An' I got me a tiddy live 'eathen
   Through buyin' supplies off 'er pa.

[1] Head-groom.

Funny an' yellow an' faithful—
    Doll in a teacup she were—
But we lived on the square, like a true-married pair,
    An' I learned about women from 'er!

Then we was shifted to Neemuch
    (Or I might ha' been keepin' 'er now),
An' I took with a shiny she-devil,
    The wife of a nigger at Mhow;
'Taught me the gipsy-folks' *bolee*;[1]
    Kind o' volcano she were,
For she knifed me one night 'cause I wished she was
        white,
    And I learned about women from 'er!

Then I come 'ome in a trooper,
    'Long of a kid o' sixteen—
'Girl from a convent at Meerut,
    The straightest I ever 'ave seen.
Love at first sight was 'er trouble,
    She didn't know what it were;
An' I wouldn't do such, 'cause I liked 'er too much,
    But—I learned about women from 'er!

I've taken my fun where I've found it,
    An' now I must pay for my fun,
For the more you 'ave known o' the others
    The less will you settle to one;
An' the end of it's sittin' and thinkin',
    An' dreamin' Hell-fires to see;
So be warned by my lot (which I know you will
        not),
    An' learn about women from me!

[1] Slang.

What did the Colonel's Lady think?
  Nobody never knew.
Somebody asked the Sergeant's Wife,
  An' she told 'em true!
When you get to a man in the case,
  They're like as a row of pins—
For the Colonel's Lady an' Judy O'Grady
  Are sisters under their skins!

'FOLLOW ME 'OME'

There was no one like 'im, 'Orse or Foot,
  Nor any o' the Guns I knew;
An' because it was so, why, o' course 'e went an' died,
  Which is just what the best men do.

  So it's knock out your pipes an' follow me!
  An' it's finish up your swipes an' follow me!
    Oh, 'ark to the big drum callin',
      Follow me—follow me 'ome!

'Is mare she neighs the 'ole day long,
  She paws the 'ole night through.
An' she won't take 'er feed 'cause o' waitin' for 'is
step,
  Which is just what a beast would do.

'Is girl she goes with a bombardier
  Before 'er month is through;
An' the banns are up in church, for she's got the beggar
hooked,
  Which is just what a girl would do.

213

We fought 'bout a dog—last week it were—
    No more than a round or two;
But I strook 'im cruel 'ard, an' I wish I 'adn't now,
    Which is just what a man can't do.

'E was all that I 'ad in the way of a friend,
    An' I've 'ad to find one new;
But I'd give my pay an' stripe for to get the beggar back,
    Which it's just too late to do!

So it's knock out your pipes an' follow me!
An' it's finish up your swipes an' follow me!
    Oh, 'ark to the fifes a-crawlin'!
        Follow me—follow me 'ome!

Take 'im away! 'E's gone where the best men go.
Take 'im away! An' the gun-wheels turnin' slow.
Take 'im away! There's more from the place 'e come.
Take 'im away, with the limber an' the drum.

For it's 'Three rounds blank' an' follow me,
An' it's 'Thirteen rank' an' follow me;
    Oh, passin' the love o' women,
        Follow me—follow me 'ome!

THE SERGEANT'S WEDDIN'

'E was warned agin 'er—
    That's what made 'im look;
She was warned agin' 'im—
    That is why she took.
Wouldn't 'ear no reason,
    'Went an' done it blind;
We know all about 'em,
    They've got all to find!

214

Cheer for the Sergeant's weddin'—
  Give 'em one cheer more!
Grey gun-'orses in the lando,
  An' a rogue is married to, etc.

What's the use o' tellin'
  'Arf the lot she's been?
'E's a bloomin' robber,
  An' 'e keeps canteen.
'Ow did 'e get 'is buggy?
  Gawd, you needn't ask!
'Made 'is forty gallon
  Out of every cask!

Watch 'im, with 'is 'air cut,
  Count us filin' by—
Won't the Colonel praise 'is
  Pop—u—lar—i—ty!
We 'ave scores to settle—
  Scores for more than beer;
She's the girl to pay 'em—
  That is why we're 'ere!

See the Chaplain thinkin'?
  See the women smile?
Twig the married winkin'
  As they take the aisle?
Keep your side-arms quiet,
  Dressin' by the Band.
Ho! You 'oly beggars,
  Cough be'ind your 'and!

Now it's done an' over,
  'Ear the organ squeak,
"Voice that breathed o'er Eden"—
  Ain't she got the cheek!

White an' laylock ribbons,
  'Think yourself so fine!
I'd pray Gawd to take yer
  'Fore I made yer mine!

Escort to the kerridge,
  Wish 'im luck, the brute!
Chuck the slippers after—
  (Pity 'tain't a boot!)
Bowin' like a lady,
  Blushin' like a lad—
'Oo would say to see 'em
  Both is rotten bad?

Cheer for the Sergeant's weddin'—
  Give 'em one cheer more!
Grey gun-'orses in the lando,
  An' a rogue is married to, etc.

THE 'EATHEN

The 'eathen in 'is blindness bows down to wood an'
    stone;
'E don't obey no orders unless they is 'is own;
'E keeps 'is side-arms awful: 'e leaves 'em all about,
An' then comes up the Regiment an' pokes the 'eathen out.

  All along o' dirtiness, all along o' mess,
  All along o' doin' things rather-more-or-less,
  All along of abby-nay,[1] kul,[2] an' hazar-ho,[3]
  Mind you keep your rifle an' yourself jus' so!

[1] Not now.
[2] To-morrow.
[3] Wait a bit.

216

The young recruit is 'aughty—'e draf's from Gawd knows
      where;
They bid 'im show 'is stockin's an' lay 'is mattress square;
'E calls it bloomin' nonsense—'e doesn't know, no more—
An' then up comes 'is Company an' kicks 'im round the
      floor!

The young recruit is 'ammered—'e takes it very hard;
'E 'angs 'is 'ead an' mutters—'e sulks about the yard;
'E talks o' 'cruel tyrants' which 'e'll swing for by-an'-
      by,
An' the others 'ears an' mocks 'im, an' the boy goes orf to
      cry.

The young recruit is silly—'e thinks o' suicide.
'E's lost 'is gutter-devil; 'e 'asn't got 'is pride;
But day by day they kicks 'im, which 'elps 'im on a bit,
Till 'e finds 'isself one mornin' with a full an' proper
      kit.

    Gettin' clear o' dirtiness, gettin' done with mess,
    Gettin' shut o' doin' things rather-more-or-less;
    Not so fond of abby-nay, kul, nor hazar-ho,
    Learns to keep 'is rifle an' 'isself jus' so!

The young recruit is 'appy—'e throws a chest to suit;
You see 'im grow mustaches; you 'ear 'im slap 'is boot.
'E learns to drop the 'bloodies' from every word 'e
      slings,
An' 'e shows an 'ealthy brisket when 'e strips for bars an'
      rings.

The cruel-tyrant-sergeants they watch 'im 'arf a year;
They watch 'im with 'is comrades, they watch 'im with 'is
      beer;

They watch 'im with the women at the regimental dance,
And the cruel-tyrant-sergeants send 'is name along for
'Lance'.

An' now 'e's 'arf o' nothin', an' all a private yet,
'Is room they up an' rags 'im to see what they will get.
They rags 'im low an' cunnin', each dirty trick they
can,
But 'e learns to sweat 'is temper an' 'e learns to sweat 'is
man.

An', last, a Colour-Sergeant, as such to be obeyed,
'E schools 'is men at cricket, 'e tells 'em on parade;
They sees 'im quick an' 'andy, uncommon set an'
smart,
An' so 'e talks to orficers which 'ave the Core at 'eart.

'E learns to do 'is watchin' without it showin' plain;
'E learns to save a dummy, an' shove 'im straight again;
'E learns to check a ranker that's buying leave to shirk;
An' 'e learns to make men like 'im so they'll learn to like
their work.

An' when it comes to marchin' he'll see their socks are
right,
An' when it comes to action 'e shows 'em how to sight.
'E knows their ways of thinkin' and just what's in their
mind;
'E knows when they are takin' on an' when they've fell
be'ind.

'E knows each talkin' corp'ral that leads a squad astray;
'E feels 'is innards 'eavin', 'is bowels givin' way;
'E sees the blue-white faces all tryin' 'ard to grin,
An' 'e stands an' waits an' suffers till it's time to cap
'em in.

An' now the hugly bullets come peckin' through the
    dust,
An' no one wants to face 'em, but every beggar must;
So, like a man in irons, which isn't glad to go,
They moves 'em off by companies uncommon stiff an'
    slow.

Of all 'is five years' schoolin' they don't remember
    much
Excep' the not retreatin', the step an' keepin' touch.
It looks like teachin' wasted when they duck an' spread an'
    'op—
But if 'e 'adn't learned 'em they'd be all about the shop.

An' now it's "'Oo goes backward?' an' now it's "'Oo comes
    on ?'
And now it's 'Get the doolies,' an' now the Captain's
    gone;
An' now it's bloody murder, but all the while they
    'ear
'Is voice, the same as barrick-drill, a-shepherdin' the
    rear.

'E's just as sick as they are, 'is 'eart is like to split,
But 'e works 'em, works 'em, works 'em till he feels 'em
    take the bit;
The rest is 'oldin' steady till the watchful bugles play,
An' 'e lifts 'em, lifts 'em, lifts 'em through the charge that
    wins the day!

   The 'eathen in 'is blindness bows down to wood an'
     stone;
   'E don't obey no orders unless they is 'is own.
   The 'eathen in 'is blindness must end where 'e began,
   But the backbone of the Army is the Non-commissioned
     Man!

Keep away from dirtiness—keep away from mess,
Don't get into doin' things rather-more-or-less!
Let's ha' done with abby-nay, kul, and hazar-ho;
Mind you keep your rifle an' yourself jus' so!

'FOR TO ADMIRE'

The Injian Ocean sets an' smiles
    So sof', so bright, so bloomin' blue;
There aren't a wave for miles an' miles
    Excep' the jiggle from the screw.
The ship is swep', the day is done,
    The bugle's gone for smoke and play;
An' black ag'in the settin' sun
    The Lascar sings, '*Hum deckty hai!*'[1]

For to admire an' for to see,
    For to be'old this world so wide—
It never done no good to me,
    But I can't drop it if I tried!

I see the sergeants pitchin' quoits,
    I 'ear the women laugh an' talk,
I spy upon the quarter-deck
    The orficers an' lydies walk.
I thinks about the things that was,
    An' leans an' looks acrost the sea,
Till, spite of all the crowded ship,
    There's no one lef' alive but me.

The things that was which I 'ave seen,
    In barrick, camp, an' action too,
I tells them over by myself,
    An' sometimes wonders if they're true;
                [1] I'm looking out.

220

For they was odd—most awful odd—
　　But all the same, now they are o'er,
There must be 'eaps o' plenty such,
　　An' if I wait I'll see some more.

Oh, I 'ave come upon the books,
　　An' frequent broke a barrick-rule,
An' stood beside an' watched myself
　　Be'avin' like a bloomin' fool.
I paid my price for findin' out,
　　Nor never grutched the price I paid,
But sat in Clink without my boots,
　　Admirin' 'ow the world was made.

Be'old a cloud upon the beam,
　　An' 'umped above the sea appears
Old Aden, like a barrick-stove
　　That no one's lit for years an' years.
I passed by that when I began,
　　An' I go 'ome the road I came,
A time-expired soldier-man
　　With six years' service to 'is name.

My girl she said, 'Oh, stay with me!'
　　My mother 'eld me to 'er breast.
They've never written none, an' so
　　They must 'ave gone with all the rest—
With all the rest which I 'ave seen
　　An' found an' known an' met along.
I cannot say the things I feel,
　　And so I sing my evenin' song:

For to admire an' for to see,
　　For to be'old this world so wide—
It never done no good to me,
　　But I can't drop it if I tried!

221

THE ABSENT-MINDED BEGGAR

When you've shouted 'Rule Britannia,' when you've
    sung 'God save the Queen,'
When you've finished killing Kruger with your mouth,
Will you kindly drop a shilling in my little tambourine
    For a gentleman in khaki ordered South?
He's an absent-minded beggar, and his weaknesses are
      great—
    But we and Paul must take him as we find him—
He is out on active service, wiping something off a slate—
    And he's left a lot of little things behind him!
Duke's son—cook's son—son of a hundred kings—
    (Fifty thousand horse and foot going to Table Bay!)
Each of 'em doing his country's work
    (and who's to look after their things?)
Pass the hat for your credit's sake,
               and pay—pay—pay!

There are girls he married secret, asking no permission to,
    For he knew he wouldn't get it if he did.
There is gas and coals and vittles, and the house-rent
    falling due,
    And it's more than rather likely there's a kid.
There are girls he walked with casual. They'll be sorry now
    he's gone,
    For an absent-minded beggar they will find him,
But it ain't the time for sermons with the winter coming
    on.
    We must help the girl that Tommy's left behind him!
Cook's son—Duke's son—son of a belted Earl—
    Son of a Lambeth publican—it's all the same to-day!
Each of 'em doing his country's work
    (and who's to look after the girl?)
Pass the hat for your credit's sake,
               and pay—pay—pay!

There are families by thousands, far too proud to beg or
	speak,
   And they'll put their sticks and bedding up the
	spout,
And they'll live on half o' nothing, paid 'em punctual once
	a week,
   'Cause the man that earns the wage is ordered
	out.
He's an absent-minded beggar, but he heard his country
	call,
   And his reg'ment didn't need to send to find
	him!
He chucked his job and joined it—so the job before
	us all
   Is to help the home that Tommy's left behind him!
Duke's job—cook's job—gardener, baronet, groom,
   Mews or palace or paper-shop, there's someone gone
	away!
Each of 'em doing his country's work
   (and who's to look after the room?)
Pass the hat for your credit's sake,
			and pay—pay—pay!

Let us manage so as, later, we can look him in the
	face,
   And tell him—what he'd very much prefer—
That, while he saved the Empire, his employer saved his
	place,
   And his mates (that's you and me) looked out for
	her.
He's an absent-minded beggar and he may forget it all,
   But we do not want his kiddies to remind him
That we sent 'em to the workhouse while their daddy
	hammered Paul,
   So we'll help the homes that Tommy left behind
	him!

223

Cook's home—Duke's home—home of a millionaire,
  (Fifty thousand horse and foot going to Table Bay!)
Each of 'em doing his country's work
  (and what have you got to spare?)
Pass the hat for your credit's sake,
                    and pay—pay—pay!

CHANT-PAGAN

(English Irregular, discharged)

Me that 'ave been what I've been—
Me that 'ave gone where I've gone—
Me that 'ave seen what I've seen—
  'Ow can I ever take on
With awful old England again,
An' 'ouses both sides of the street,
And 'edges two sides of the lane,
And the parson an' gentry between,
An' touchin' my 'at when we meet—
  Me that 'ave been what I've been?

Me that 'ave watched 'arf a world
'Eave up all shiny with dew,
Kopje on kop to the sun,
An' as soon as the mist let 'em through
Our 'elios winkin' like fun—
Three sides of a ninety-mile square,
Over valleys as big as a shire—
'*Are ye there? Are ye there? Are ye there?*'
An' then the blind drum of our fire . . .
An' I'm rollin' 'is lawns for the Squire,
                              Me!

224

Me that 'ave rode through the dark
Forty mile, often, on end,
Along the Ma'ollisberg Range,
With only the stars for my mark
An' only the night for my friend,
An' things runnin' off as you pass,
An' things jumpin' up in the grass,
An' the silence, the shine an' the size
Of the 'igh, unexpressible skies—
I am takin' some letters almost
As much as a mile to the post,
An' 'mind you come back with the change!'
                                    Me!

Me that saw Barberton took
When we dropped through the clouds on their
    'ead,
An' they 'ove the guns over and fled—
Me that was through Di'mond 'Ill,
An' Pieters an' Springs an' Belfast—
From Dundee to Vereeniging all—
Me that stuck out to the last
(An' five bloomin' bars on my chest)—
I am doin' my Sunday-school best,
By the 'elp of the Squire and 'is wife
(Not to mention the 'ousemaid an' cook),
To come in an' 'ands up an' be still,
An' honestly work for my bread,
My livin' in that state of life
To which it shall please God to call
                                    Me!

Me that 'ave followed my trade
In the place where the Lightnin's are made;
'Twixt the Rains and the Sun and the Moon—
Me that lay down an' got up

Three years with the sky for my roof—
That 'ave ridden my 'unger an' thirst
Six thousand raw mile on the hoof,
With the Vaal and the Orange for cup,
An' the Brandwater Basin for dish,—
Oh! it's 'ard to be'ave as they wish
(Too 'ard, an' a little too soon),
I'll 'ave to think over it first—

      Me!

I will arise an' get 'ence—
I will trek South and make sure
If it's only my fancy or not
That the sunshine of England is pale,
And the breezes of England are stale,
An' there's somethin' gone small with the lot.
For *I* know of a sun an' a wind,
An' some plains and a mountain be'ind,
An' some graves by a barb-wire fence,
An' a Dutchman I've fought 'oo might give
Me a job were I ever inclined
To look in an' offsaddle an' live
Where there's neither a road nor a tree—
But only my Maker an' me,
And I think it will kill me or cure,
So I think I will go there an' see.

      Me!

BOOTS

(*Infantry Columns*)

We're foot—slog—slog—slog—sloggin' over Africa—
Foot—foot—foot—foot—sloggin' over Africa—
(Boots—boots—boots—boots—movin' up and down
again!)
There's no discharge in the war!

Seven—six—eleven—five—nine-an'-twenty mile to-day—
Four—eleven—seventeen—thirty-two the day before—
(Boots—boots—boots—boots—movin' up and down
again!)
There's no discharge in the war!

Don't—don't—don't—don't—look at what's in front of
you.
(Boots—boots—boots—boots—movin' up an' down
again);
Men—men—men—men—men go mad with watchin' 'em,
An' there's no discharge in the war!

Try—try—try—try—to think o' something different—
Oh—my—God—keep—me from goin' lunatic!
(Boots—boots—boots—boots—movin' up an' down
again!)
There's no discharge in the war!

Count—count—count—count—the bullets in the bando-
liers.
If—your—eyes—drop—they will get atop o' you!
(Boots—boots—boots—boots—movin' up and down
again)—
There's no discharge in the war!

We—can—stick—out—'unger, thirst, an' weariness,
But—not—not—not—not the chronic sight of 'em—
Boots—boots—boots—boots—movin' up an' down
    again,
        An' there's no discharge in the war!

'Tain't—so—bad—by—day because o' company,
But night—brings—long—strings—o' forty thousand
    million
Boots—boots—boots—boots—movin' up an' down
    again.
        There's no discharge in the war!

I—'ave—marched—six—weeks in 'Ell an' certify
It—is—not—fire—devils, dark, or anything,
But boots—boots—boots—boots—movin' up an' down
    again,
        An' there's no discharge in the war!

THE MARRIED MAN

(*Reservist of the Line*)

The bachelor 'e fights for one
  As joyful as can be;
But the married man don't call it fun,
  Because 'e fights for three—
For 'Im an' 'Er an' It
  (An' Two an' One make Three)
'E wants to finish 'is little bit,
  An' 'e wants to go 'ome to 'is tea!

228

The bachelor pokes up 'is 'ead
　　To see if you are gone;
But the married man lies down instead,
　　An' waits till the sights come on,
For 'Im an' 'Er an' a hit
　　(Direct or ricochee)
'E wants to finish 'is little bit,
　　An' 'e wants to go 'ome to 'is tea.

The bachelor will miss you clear
　　To fight another day;
But the married man, 'e says 'No fear!'
　　'E wants you out of the way
Of 'Im an' 'Er an' It
　　(An' 'is road to 'is farm or the sea),
'E wants to finish 'is little bit,
　　An' 'e wants to go 'ome to 'is tea.

The bachelor 'e fights 'is fight
　　An' stretches out an' snores;
But the married man sits up all night—
　　For 'e don't like out-o'-doors.
'E'll strain an' listen an' peer
　　An' give the first alarm—
For the sake o' the breathin' 'e's used to 'ear,
　　An' the 'ead on the thick of 'is arm.

The bachelor may risk 'is 'ide
　　To 'elp you when you're downed;
But the married man will wait beside
　　Till the ambulance comes round.
'E'll take your 'ome address
　　An' all you've time to say,
Or if 'e sees there's 'ope, 'e'll press
　　Your art'ry 'alf the day—

For 'Im an' 'Er an' It
  (An' One from Three leaves Two),
For 'e knows you wanted to finish your bit,
  An' 'e knows 'oo's wantin' you.
Yes, 'Im an' 'Er an' It
  (Our 'oly One in Three),
We're all of us anxious to finish our bit,
  An' we want to get 'ome to our tea!

Yes, It an' 'Er an' 'Im,
  Which often makes me think
The married man must sink or swim
  An'—'e can't afford to sink!
Oh, 'Im an' It an' 'Er
  Since Adam an' Eve began!
So I'd rather fight with the bachel*er*
  An' be nursed by the married man!

STELLENBOSCH

(*Composite Columns*)

The General 'eard the firin' on the flank,
  An' 'e sent a mounted man to bring 'im back
The silly, pushin' person's name an' rank
  'Oo'd dared to answer Brother Boer's attack:
For there might 'ave been a serious engagement,
  An' 'e might 'ave wasted 'alf a dozen men;
So 'e ordered 'im to stop 'is operations round the
    kopjes,
  An' 'e told 'im off before the Staff at ten!

    And it all goes into the laundry,
    But it never comes out in the wash,

'Ow we're sugared about by the old men
('Eavy-sterned amateur old men!)
That 'amper an' 'inder an' scold men
For fear o' Stellenbosch![1]

The General 'ad 'produced a great effect',
   The General 'ad the country cleared—almost;
The General ''ad no reason to expect',
   And the Boers 'ad us bloomin' well on toast!
For we might 'ave crossed the drift before the twilight,
   Instead o' sitting down an' takin' root;
But we was not allowed, so the Boojers scooped the crowd,
   To the last survivin' bandolier an' boot.

The General saw the farm'ouse in 'is rear,
   With its stoep so nicely shaded from the sun;
Sez 'e, 'I'll pitch my tabernacle 'ere,'
   An' 'e kept us muckin' round till 'e 'ad done.
For 'e might 'ave caught the confluent pneumonia
   From sleepin' in his gaiters in the dew;
So 'e took a book an' dozed while the other columns
     closed,
   And De Wet's commando out an' trickled through!

The General saw the mountain-range ahead,
   With their 'elios showin' saucy on the 'eight,
So 'e 'eld us to the level ground instead,
   An' telegraphed the Boojers wouldn't fight.
For 'e might 'ave gone an' sprayed 'em with a pompom,
   Or 'e might 'ave slung a squadron out to see—
But 'e wasn't takin' chances in them 'igh an' 'ostile
     kranzes—
   He was markin' time to earn a K.C.B.

[1] The more notoriously incompetent commanders used to be sent to
the town of Stellenbosch, which name became a verb.

The General got 'is decorations thick
  (The men that backed 'is lies could not complain),
The Staff 'ad D.S.O.'s till we was sick,
  An' the soldier—'ad the work to do again!
For 'e might 'ave known the District was an 'otbed,
  Instead of 'andin' over, upside-down,
To a man 'oo 'ad to fight 'alf a year to put it right,
  While the General sat an' slandered 'im in town!

      An' it all went into the laundry,
      But it never came out in the wash.
      We were sugared about by the old men
      (Panicky, perishin' old men)
      That 'amper an' 'inder an' scold men
      For fear o' Stellenbosch!

PIET

(*Regular of the Line*)

I do not love my Empire's foes,
  Nor call 'em angels; still,
What *is* the sense of 'ating those
  'Oom you are paid to kill?
So, barrin' all that foreign lot
  Which only joined for spite,
Myself, I'd just as soon as not
  Respect the man I fight.
      Ah, there, Piet!—'is trousies to 'is knees,
      'Is coat-tails lyin' level in the bullet-sprinkled breeze;
      'E does not lose 'is rifle an' 'e does not lose 'is
        seat.
      I've known a lot o' people ride a dam' sight worse
        than Piet.

I've 'eard 'im cryin' from the ground
  Like Abel's blood of old,
An' skirmished out to look, an' found
  The beggar nearly cold.
I've waited on till 'e was dead
  (Which couldn't 'elp 'im much),
But many grateful things 'e's said
  To me for doin' such.
    Ah, there, Piet! whose time 'as come to die,
    'Is carcase past rebellion, but 'is eyes inquirin' why.
    Though dressed in stolen uniform with badge o' rank
      complete,
    I've known a lot o' fellers go a dam' sight worse than
      Piet.

An' when there wasn't aught to do
  But camp and cattle-guards,
I've fought with 'im the 'ole day through
  At fifteen 'undred yards;
Long afternoons o' lying still,
  An' 'earin' as you lay
The bullets swish from 'ill to 'ill
  Like scythes among the 'ay.
    Ah, there, Piet!—be'ind 'is stony kop—
    With 'is Boer bread an' biltong,[1] an' 'is flask of awful
      Dop;[2]
    'Is Mauser for amusement an' 'is pony for retreat,
    I've known a lot o' fellers shoot a dam' sight worse
      than Piet.

He's shoved 'is rifle 'neath my nose
  Before I'd time to think,
An' borrowed all my Sunday clo'es
  An' sent me 'ome in pink;

[1] Dried meat.   [2] Cape brandy.

An' I 'ave crept (Lord, 'ow I've crept!)
 On 'ands an' knees I've gone,
And spoored and floored and caught and kept
 An' sent him to Ceylon![1]
  Ah, there, Piet!—you've sold me many a pup,
  When week on week alternate it was you an' me
   "'ands up!'
  But though I never made *you* walk man-naked in the
   'eat,
  I've known a lot of fellows stalk a dam' sight worse
   than Piet.

From Plewman's to Marabastad,
 From Ookiep to De Aar,
Me an' my trusty friend 'ave 'ad,
 As you might say, a war;
But seein' what both parties done
 Before 'e owned defeat,
I ain't more proud of 'avin' won
 Than I am pleased with Piet.
  Ah, there, Piet!—picked up be'ind the drive!
  The wonder wasn't 'ow 'e fought, but 'ow 'e kep'
   alive,
  With nothin' in 'is belly, on 'is back, or to 'is feet—
  I've known a lot o' men behave a dam' sight worse
   than Piet.

No more I'll 'ear 'is rifle crack
 Along the block'ouse fence—
The beggar's on the peaceful tack,
 Regardless of expense;
For countin' what 'e eats an' draws,
 An' gifts an' loans as well,
'E's gettin' 'alf the Earth, because
 'E didn't give us 'Ell!

---

[1] One of the camps for prisoners of this war was in Ceylon.

Ah, there, Piet! with your brand-new English plough,
Your gratis tents an' cattle, an' your most ungrateful
frow,
You've made the British taxpayer rebuild your
country-seat—
I've known some pet battalions charge a dam' sight
less than Piet.

UBIQUE

(*Royal Artillery*)

There is a word you often see, pronounce it as you
may—
'You bike,' 'you bykwee,' 'ubbikwe'—alludin' to R.A.
It serves 'Orse, Field, an' Garrison as motto for a crest;
An' when you've found out all it means I'll tell you 'alf
the rest.

Ubique means the long-range Krupp be'ind the low-range
'ill--
Ubique means you'll pick it up an', while you do, stand
still.
Ubique means you've caught the flash an' timed it by the
sound.
Ubique means five gunners' 'ash before you've loosed a
round.

Ubique means Blue Fuse,[1] an' make the 'ole to sink the
trail.
Ubique means stand up an' take the Mauser's 'alf-mile 'ail.
Ubique means the crazy team not God nor man can 'old.
Ubique means that 'orse's scream which turns your innards
cold!

[1] Extreme range.

235

Ubique means 'Bank, 'Olborn, Bank—a penny all the
way'—
The soothin', jingle-bump-an'-clank from day to peaceful
day.
Ubique means 'They've caught De Wet, an' now we shan't
be long.'
Ubique means 'I much regret, the beggar's goin' strong!'

Ubique means the tearin' drift where, breech-blocks
jammed with mud,
The khaki muzzles duck an' lift across the khaki flood.
Ubique means the dancing plain that changes rocks to
Boers.
Ubique means mirage again an' shellin' all outdoors.

Ubique means 'Entrain at once for Grootdefeatfontein.'
Ubique means 'Off-load your guns'—at midnight in the
rain!
Ubique means 'More mounted men. Return all guns to
store.'
Ubique means the R.A.M.R. Infantillery Corps.[1]

Ubique means that warnin' grunt the perished linesman
knows,
When o'er 'is strung an' sufferin' front the shrapnel sprays
'is foes;
An' as their firin' dies away the 'usky whisper runs
From lips that 'aven't drunk all day: 'The Guns! Thank
Gawd, the Guns!'

Extreme, depressed, point-blank or short, end-first or
any'ow,

[1] The Royal Artillery Mounted Rifles—when mounted infantry were
badly needed.

From Colesberg Kop to Quagga's Poort—from Ninety-
    Nine till now—
By what I've 'eard the others tell an' I in spots 'ave seen,
There's nothin' this side 'Eaven or 'Ell Ubique doesn't
    mean!

THE RETURN

(*All Arms*)

Peace is declared, an' I return
    To 'Ackneystadt, but not the same;
Things 'ave transpired which made me learn
    The size and meanin' of the game.
I did no more than others did,
    I don't know where the change began.
I started as a average kid,
    I finished as a thinkin' man.

If England was what England seems,
    An' not the England of our dreams,
But only putty, brass, an' paint,
    'Ow quick we'd drop 'er! But she ain't!

Before my gappin' mouth could speak
    I 'eard it in my comrade's tone.
I saw it on my neighbour's cheek
    Before I felt it flush my own.
An' last it come to me—not pride,
    Nor yet conceit, but on the 'ole
(If such a term may be applied),
    The makin's of a bloomin' soul.

Rivers at night that cluck an' jeer,
    Plains which the moonshine turns to sea,
Mountains which never let you near,
    An' stars to all eternity;

237

An' the quick-breathin' dark that fills
   The 'ollows of the wilderness,
When the wind worries through the 'ills—
   These may 'ave taught me more or less.

Towns without people, ten times took,
   An' ten times left an' burned at last;
An' starving dogs that come to look
   For owners when a column passed;
An' quiet, 'omesick talks between
   Men, met by night, you never knew
Until—'is face—by shellfire seen—
   Once—an' struck off. *They* taught me too.

The day's lay-out—the mornin' sun
   Beneath your 'at-brim as you sight;
The dinner-'ush from noon till one,
   An' the full roar that lasts till night;
An' the pore dead that look so old
   An' was so young an hour ago,
An' legs tied down before they're cold—
   These are the things which make you know.

Also Time runnin' into years—
   A thousand Places left be'ind—
An' Men from both two 'emispheres
   Discussin' things of every kind;
So much more near than I 'ad known,
   So much more great than I 'ad guessed—
An' me, like all the rest, alone—
   But reachin' out to all the rest!

So 'ath it come to me—not pride,
   Nor yet conceit, but on the 'ole
(If such a term may be applied),
   The makin's of a bloomin' soul.

But now, discharged, I fall away
   To do with little things again. . . .
Gawd, 'oo knows all I cannot say,
   Look after me in Thamesfontein![1]

     If England was what England seems,
       An' not the England of our dreams,
     But only putty, brass, an' paint,
       'Ow quick we'd chuck 'er! But she ain't!

'CITIES AND THRONES AND POWERS'

('A Centurion of the Thirtieth'—*Puck of Pook's Hill*)

Cities and Thrones and Powers
   Stand in Time's eye,
Almost as long as flowers,
   Which daily die:
But, as new buds put forth
   To glad new men,
Out of the spent and unconsidered Earth
   The Cities rise again.

This season's Daffodil,
   She never hears
What change, what chance, what chill,
   Cut down last year's;
But with bold countenance,
   And knowledge small,
Esteems her seven days' continuance
   To be perpetual.

[1] London.

So Time that is o'er-kind
  To all that be,
Ordains us e'en as blind,
  As bold as she:
That in our very death,
  And burial sure,
Shadow to shadow, well persuaded, saith,
  'See how our works endure!'

THE RECALL

('An Habitation Enforced'—*Actions and Reactions*)

I am the land of their fathers.
In me the virtue stays.
I will bring back my children,
After certain days.

Under their feet in the grasses
My clinging magic runs.
They shall return as strangers.
They shall remain as sons.

Over their heads in the branches
Of their new-bought, ancient trees,
I weave an incantation
And draw them to my knees.

Scent of smoke in the evening,
Smell of rain in the night—
The hours, the days and the seasons,
Order their souls aright,

Till I make plain the meaning
Of all my thousand years—
Till I fill their hearts with knowledge,
While I fill their eyes with tears.

240

PUCK'S SONG

(*Enlarged from 'Puck of Pook's Hill'*)

See you the ferny ride that steals
Into the oak-woods far?
O that was whence they hewed the keels
That rolled to Trafalgar.

And mark you where the ivy clings
To Bayham's mouldering walls?
O there we cast the stout railings
That stand around St. Paul's.

See you the dimpled track that runs
All hollow through the wheat?
O that was where they hauled the guns
That smote King Philip's fleet.

(Out of the Weald, the secret Weald,
Men sent in ancient years
The horse-shoes red at Flodden Field,
The arrows at Poitiers!)

See you our little mill that clacks,
So busy by the brook?
She has ground her corn and paid her tax
Ever since Domesday Book.

See you our stilly woods of oak,
And the dread ditch beside?
O that was where the Saxons broke
On the day that Harold died.

See you the windy levels spread
About the gates of Rye?
O that was where the Northmen fled,
When Alfred's ships came by.

241

See you our pastures wide and lone,
Where the red oxen browse?
O there was a City thronged and known,
Ere London boasted a house.

And see you, after rain, the trace
Of mound and ditch and wall?
O that was a Legion's camping-place,
When Caesar sailed from Gaul.

And see you marks that show and fade,
Like shadows on the Downs?
O they are the lines the Flint Men made,
To guard their wondrous towns.

Trackway and Camp and City lost,
Salt Marsh where now is corn—
Old Wars, old Peace, old Arts that cease,
And so was England born!

She is not any common Earth,
Water or wood or air,
But Merlin's Isle of Gramarye,
Where you and I will fare!

THE WAY THROUGH THE WOODS

('Marklake Witches'—*Rewards and Fairies*)

They shut the road through the woods
  Seventy years ago.
Weather and rain have undone it again,
And now you would never know
There was once a road through the woods
Before they planted the trees.

It is underneath the coppice and heath
And the thin anemones.
Only the keeper sees
That, where the ring-dove broods,
And the badgers roll at ease,
There was once a road through the woods.

Yet, if you enter the woods
Of a summer evening late,
When the night-air cools on the trout-ringed pools
Where the otter whistles his mate,
(They fear not men in the woods,
Because they see so few.)
You will hear the beat of a horse's feet,
And the swish of a skirt in the dew,
Steadily cantering through
The misty solitudes,
As though they perfectly knew
The old lost road through the woods. . . .
But there is no road through the woods.

A THREE-PART SONG

(' "Dymchurch Flit" '—*Puck of Pook's Hill*)

I'm just in love with all these three,
  The Weald and the Marsh and the Down countree.
Nor I don't know which I love the most,
The Weald or the Marsh or the white Chalk coast!

I've buried my heart in a ferny hill,
Twix' a liddle low shaw an' a great high gill.
Oh, hop-bine yaller an' wood-smoke blue,
I reckon you'll keep her middling true!

I've loosed my mind for to out and run
On a Marsh that was old when Kings begun.
Oh, Romney Level and Brenzett reeds,
I reckon you know what my mind needs!

I've given my soul to the Southdown grass,
And sheep-bells tinkled where you pass.
Oh, Firle an' Ditchling an' sails at sea,
I reckon you keep my soul for me!

THE RUN OF THE DOWNS

('The Knife and the Naked Chalk'—*Rewards and Fairies*)

The Weald is good, the Downs are best—
I'll give you the run of 'em, East to West.
Beachy Head and Winddoor Hill,
They were once and they are still.
Firle, Mount Caburn and Mount Harry
Go back as far as sums'll carry.
Ditchling Beacon and Chanctonbury Ring,
They have looked on many a thing,
And what those two have missed between 'em,
I reckon Truleigh Hill has seen 'em.
Highden, Bignor and Duncton Down
Knew Old England before the Crown.
Linch Down, Treyford and Sunwood
Knew Old England before the Flood;
And when you end on the Hampshire side—
Butser's old as Time and Tide.
The Downs are sheep, the Weald is corn,
You be glad you are Sussex born!

SIR RICHARD'S SONG

(A.D. 1066)

('Young Men at the Manor'—*Puck of Pook's Hill*)

I followed my Duke ere I was a lover,
To take from England fief and fee;
But now this game is the other way over—
　　But now England hath taken me!

I had my horse, my shield and banner,
　　And a boy's heart, so whole and free;
But now I sing in another manner—
　　But now England hath taken me!

As for my Father in his tower,
　　Asking news of my ship at sea,
He will remember his own hour—
　　Tell him England hath taken me!

As for my Mother in her bower,
　　That rules my Father so cunningly,
She will remember a maiden's power—
　　Tell her England hath taken me!

As for my Brother in Rouen City,
　　A nimble and naughty page is he,
But he will come to suffer and pity—
　　Tell him England hath taken me!

As for my little Sister waiting
　　In the pleasant orchards of Normandie,
Tell her youth is the time for mating—
　　Tell her England hath taken me!

As for my comrades in camp and highway,
  That lift their eyebrows scornfully,
Tell them their way is not my way—
  Tell them England hath taken me!

Kings and Princes and Barons famèd,
  Knights and Captains in your degree;
Hear me a little before I am blamèd—
  Seeing England hath taken me!

Howso great man's strength be reckoned,
  There are two things he cannot flee.
Love is the first, and Death is the second—
  And Love in England hath taken me!

A TREE SONG

(A.D. 1200)

('Weland's Sword'—*Puck of Pook's Hill*)

Of all the trees that grow so fair,
  Old England to adorn,
Greater are none beneath the Sun
  Than Oak, and Ash, and Thorn.
Sing Oak, and Ash, and Thorn, good sirs,
  (All of a Midsummer morn!)
Surely we sing no little thing
  In Oak, and Ash, and Thorn!

Oak of the Clay lived many a day
  Or ever Æneas began.
Ash of the Loam was a lady at home
  When Brut was an outlaw man.

246

Thorn of the Down saw New Troy Town
  (From which was London born);
Witness hereby the ancientry
  Of Oak, and Ash, and Thorn!

Yew that is old in churchyard-mould,
  He breedeth a mighty bow.
Alder for shoes do wise men choose,
  And beech for cups also.
But when ye have killed, and your bowl is spilled,
  And your shoes are clean outworn,
Back ye must speed for all that ye need
  To Oak, and Ash, and Thorn!

Ellum she hateth mankind, and waiteth
  Till every gust be laid
To drop a limb on the head of him
  That anyway trusts her shade.
But whether a lad be sober or sad,
  Or mellow with ale from the horn,
He will take no wrong when he lieth along
  'Neath Oak, and Ash, and Thorn!

Oh, do not tell the Priest our plight,
  Or he would call it a sin;
But—we have been out in the woods all night,
  A-conjuring Summer in!
And we bring you news by word of mouth—
  Good news for cattle and corn—
Now is the Sun come up from the South
  With Oak, and Ash, and Thorn!

Sing Oak, and Ash, and Thorn, good sirs
  (All of a Midsummer morn)!
England shall bide till Judgment Tide
  By Oak, and Ash, and Thorn!

A CHARM

(Introduction to 'Rewards and Fairies')

Take of English earth as much
  As either hand may rightly clutch.
In the taking of it breathe
Prayer for all who lie beneath.
Not the great nor well-bespoke,
But the mere uncounted folk
Of whose life and death is none
Report or lamentation.
    Lay that earth upon thy heart,
    And thy sickness shall depart!

It shall sweeten and make whole
Fevered breath and festered soul.
It shall mightily restrain
Over-busied hand and brain.
It shall ease thy mortal strife
'Gainst the immortal woe of life,
Till thyself, restored, shall prove
By what grace the Heavens do move.

Take of English flowers these—
Spring's full-facèd primroses,
Summer's wild wide-hearted rose,
Autumn's wall-flower of the close,
And, thy darkness to illume,
Winter's bee-thronged ivy-bloom.
Seek and serve them where they bide
From Candlemas to Christmas-tide,
    For these simples, used aright,
    Can restore a failing sight.

These shall cleanse and purify
Webbed and inward-turning eye;

These shall show thee treasure hid
Thy familiar fields amid;
And reveal (which is thy need)
Every man a King indeed!

CHAPTER HEADINGS

PLAIN TALES FROM THE HILLS

Look, you have cast out Love! What Gods are these
    You bid me please?
The Three in One, the One in Three? Not so!
    To my own Gods I go.
It may be they shall give me greater ease
Than your cold Christ and tangled Trinities.

Lispeth.

When the earth was sick and the skies were grey,
    And the woods were rotted with rain,
The Dead Man rode through the autumn day
    To visit his love again.

His love she neither saw nor heard,
    So heavy was her shame;
And tho' the babe within her stirred
    She knew not that he came.

The Other Man.

Cry 'Murder' in the market-place, and each
Will turn upon his neighbour anxious eyes
Asking: 'Art thou the man?' We hunted Cain
Some centuries ago across the world.
This bred the fear our own misdeeds maintain
To-day.

His Wedded Wife.

Go, stalk the red deer o'er the heather,
Ride, follow the fox if you can!
But, for pleasure and profit together,
Allow me the hunting of Man—
The chase of the Human, the search for the Soul
To its ruin—the hunting of Man.

Pig.

''Stopped in the straight when the race was his own—
Look at him cutting it—cur to the bone!'
Ask ere the youngster be rated and chidden
What did he carry and how was he ridden?
Maybe they used him too much at the start.
Maybe Fate's weight-cloth is breaking his heart.

In the Pride of his Youth.

'And some are sulky, while some will plunge.
(*So ho! Steady! Stand still, you!*)
Some you must gentle, and some you must lunge.
(*There! There! Who wants to kill you?*)
Some—there are losses in every trade—
Will break their hearts ere bitted and made,
Will fight like fiends as the rope cuts hard,
And die dumb-mad in the breaking-yard.'

Thrown Away.

The World hath set its heavy yoke
Upon the old white-bearded folk
Who strive to please the King.
God's mercy is upon the young,
God's wisdom in the baby tongue
That fears not anything.

Tods' Amendment.

Not though you die to-night, O Sweet, and wail,
A spectre at my door,
Shall mortal Fear make Love immortal fail—
I shall but love you more,

250

Who, from Death's House returning, give me still
One moment's comfort in my matchless ill.
                                        By Word of Mouth.

They burnt a corpse upon the sand—
The light shone out afar;
It guided home the plunging dhows
That beat from Zanzibar.
Spirit of Fire, where'er Thy altars rise,
Thou art the Light of Guidance to our eyes!
                                        In Error.

Ride with an idle whip, ride with an unused heel,
But, once in a way, there will come a day
When the colt must be taught to feel
The lash that falls, and the curb that galls, and the sting of
     the rowelled steel.
                          The Conversion of Aurelian McGoggin.

It was not in the open fight
We threw away the sword,
But in the lonely watching
In the darkness by the ford.
The waters lapped, the night-wind blew,
Full-armed the Fear was born and grew,
And we were flying ere we knew
From panic in the night.
                              The Rout of the White Hussars.

In the daytime, when she moved about me,
In the night, when she was sleeping at my side,—
I was wearied, I was wearied of her presence.
Day by day and night by night I grew to hate her—
Would God that she or I had died!
                              The Bronckhorst Divorce Case.

251

A stone's throw out on either hand
From that well-ordered road we tread,
And all the world is wild and strange;
Churel[1] and ghoul and Djinn and sprite
Shall bear us company to-night,
For we have reached the Oldest Land
Wherein the Powers of Darkness range.

In the House of Suddhoo.

To-night, God knows what thing shall tide,
The Earth is racked and fain—
Expectant, sleepless, open-eyed;
And we, who from the Earth were made,
Thrill with our Mother's pain.

False Dawn.

Pit where the buffalo cooled his hide,
By the hot sun emptied, and blistered and dried;
Log in the plume-grass, hidden and lone;
Bund where the earth-rat's mounds are strown;
Cave in the bank where the sly stream steals;
Aloe that stabs at the belly and heels,
Jump if you dare on a steed untried—
Safer it is to go wide—go wide!
Hark, from in front where the best men ride:—
'Pull to the off, boys! Wide! Go wide!'

Cupid's Arrows.

He drank strong waters and his speech was coarse;
He purchased raiment and forbore to pay;
He stuck a trusting junior with a horse,
And won gymkhanas in a doubtful way.
Then, 'twixt a vice and folly, turned aside
To do good deeds—and straight to cloak them, lied.

A Bank Fraud.

[1] The ghost of a woman who has died in childbirth.

252

Thus, for a season, they fought it fair—
 She and his cousin May—
Tactful, talented, debonair,
 Decorous foes were they;
But never can battle of man compare
With merciless feminine fray.

The Rescue of Pluffles.

Then a pile of heads he laid—
 Thirty thousand heaped on high—
All to please the Kafir maid
 Where the Oxus rippled by.
Grimly spake Atulla Khan:—
 'Love hath made this thing a Man.'

His Chance in Life.

Rosicrucian subtleties
In the Orient had rise.
Ye may find their teachers still
Under Jacatâlâ's Hill.
Seek ye Bombast Paracelsus,
Read what Fludd the Seeker tells us
Of the Dominant that runs
Through the cycle of the Suns.
Read my story last and see
Luna at her apogee.

Consequences.

So we loosed a bloomin' volley
 An' we made the beggars cut,
An' when our pooch was emptied out
 We used the bloomin' butt.
Ho! My! Don't you come anigh
When Tommy is a-playin' with the bay'nit an' the butt!

The Taking of Lungtungpen.

253

Pleasant it is for the Little Tin Gods
When great Jove nods;
But Little Tin Gods make their little mistakes
In missing the hour when great Jove wakes.

A Germ-Destroyer.

There is a tide in the affairs of men
Which, taken any way you please, is bad,
And strands them in forsaken guts and creeks
No decent soul would think of visiting.
You cannot stop the tide; but, now and then,
You may arrest some rash adventurer,
Who—h'm—will hardly thank you for your pains.

Kidnapped.

While the snaffle holds or the long-neck stings,
While the big beam tilts or the last bell rings,
While horses are horses to train and to race,
Then women and wine take a second place
        For me—for me—
        While a short 'ten-three'
Has a field to squander or fence to face.

The Broken-Link Handicap.

Little Blind Fish, thou art marvellous wise!
Little Blind Fish, who put out thy eyes?
Open thy ears while I whisper my wish.
Bring me a lover, thou little Blind Fish!

The Bisara of Pooree.

254

COLD IRON

('Cold Iron'—*Rewards and Fairies*)

'*Gold is for the mistress—silver for the maid—*
  Copper for the craftsman cunning at his trade.'
'Good!' said the Baron, sitting in his hall,
'But Iron—Cold Iron—is master of them all.'

So he made rebellion 'gainst the King his liege,
Camped before his citadel and summoned it to siege.
'Nay!' said the cannoneer on the castle wall,
'But Iron—Cold Iron—shall be master of you all!'

Woe for the Baron and his knights so strong,
When the cruel cannon-balls laid 'em all along;
He was taken prisoner, he was cast in thrall,
And Iron—Cold Iron—was master of it all!

Yet his King spake kindly (ah, how kind a Lord!)
'What if I release thee now and give thee back thy
        sword?'
'Nay!' said the Baron, 'mock not at my fall,
For Iron—Cold Iron—is master of men all.'

'*Tears are for the craven, prayers are for the clown—*
Halters for the silly neck that cannot keep a crown.'
'As my loss is grievous, so my hope is small,
For Iron—Cold Iron—must be master of men all!'

Yet his King made answer (few such Kings there be!)
'Here is Bread and here is Wine—sit and sup with me.
Eat and drink in Mary's Name, the whiles I do recall
How Iron—Cold Iron—can be master of men all!'

He took the Wine and blessed it. He blessed and break
    the Bread.
With His own Hands He served Them, and presently He
    said:
'See! These Hands they pierced with nails, outside My
    city wall,
Show Iron—Cold Iron—to be master of men all.

'Wounds are for the desperate, blows are for the strong.
Balm and oil for weary hearts all cut and bruised with
    wrong.
I forgive thy treason—I redeem thy fall—
For Iron—Cold Iron—must be master of men all!'

Crowns are for the valiant—sceptres for the bold!
Thrones and powers for mighty men who dare to take and
    hold!'
'Nay!' said the Baron, kneeling in his hall,
'But Iron—Cold Iron—is master of men all!
Iron out of Calvary is master of men all!'

'MY NEW-CUT ASHLAR'

(*L'Envoi to 'Life's Handicap'*)

My new-cut ashlar takes the light
    Where crimson-blank the windows flare.
By my own work before the night,
Great Overseer, I make my prayer.

If there be good in that I wrought
Thy Hand compelled it, Master, Thine—
Where I have failed to meet Thy Thought
    know, through Thee, the blame was mine.

256

One instant's toil to Thee denied
Stands all Eternity's offence.
Of that I did with Thee to guide,
To Thee, through Thee, be excellence.

The depth and dream of my desire,
The bitter paths wherein I stray—
Thou knowest Who hast made the Fire,
Thou knowest Who hast made the Clay.

Who, lest all thought of Eden fade,
Bring'st Eden to the craftsman's brain—
Godlike to muse o'er his own Trade
And manlike stand with God again!

One stone the more swings into place
In that dread Temple of Thy worth.
It is enough that, through Thy Grace,
I saw nought common on Thy Earth.

Take not that vision from my ken—
Oh, whatsoe'er may spoil or speed.
Help me to need no aid from men
That I may help such men as need!

'NON NOBIS DOMINE!'

(Written for 'The Pageant of Parliament,' 1934)

*N*on *nobis Domine!*—
Not unto us, O Lord!
The Praise or Glory be
Of any deed or word;

257

For in Thy Judgment lies
   To crown or bring to nought
All knowledge or device
   That Man has reached or wrought.

And we confess our blame—
   How all too high we hold
That noise which men call Fame,
   That dross which men call Gold.
For these we undergo
   Our hot and godless days,
But in our hearts we know
   Not unto us the Praise.

O Power by Whom we live—
   Creator, Judge, and Friend,
Upholdingly forgive
   Nor fail us at the end:
But grant us well to see
   In all our piteous ways—
Non nobis Domine!—
   Not unto us the Praise!

THE WASTER

1930

From the date that the doors of his prep-school close
   On the lonely little son
He is taught by precept, insult, and blows
   The Things that Are Never Done.
Year after year, without favour or fear,
   From seven to twenty-two,
His keepers insist he shall learn the list
   Of the things no fellow can do.

(They are not so strict with the average Pict
    And it isn't set to, etc.)

For this and not for the profit it brings
    Or the good of his fellow-kind
He is and suffers unspeakable things
    In body and soul and mind.
But the net result of that Primitive Cult,
    Whatever else may be won,
Is definite knowledge ere leaving College
    Of the Things that Are Never Done.
(An interdict which is strange to the Pict
    And was never revealed to, etc.)

Slack by training and slow by birth,
    Only quick to despise,
Largely assessing his neighbour's worth
    By the hue of his socks or ties,
A loafer-in-grain, his foes maintain,
    And how shall we combat their view
When, atop of his natural sloth, he holds
    There are Things no Fellow can do?
(Which is why he is licked from the first by the Pict
    And left at the post by, etc.)

HARP SONG OF THE DANE WOMEN

('The Knights of the Joyous Venture'—
Puck of Pook's Hill)

What is a woman that you forsake her,
    And the hearth-fire and the home-acre,
To go with the old grey Widow-maker?

She has no house to lay a guest in—
But one chill bed for all to rest in,
That the pale suns and the stray bergs nest in.

She has no strong white arms to fold you,
But the ten-times-fingering weed to hold you—
Out on the rocks where the tide has rolled you.

Yet, when the signs of summer thicken,
And the ice breaks, and the birch-buds quicken,
Yearly you turn from our side, and sicken—

Sicken again for the shouts and the slaughters.
You steal away to the lapping waters,
And look at your ship in her winter-quarters.

You forget our mirth, and talk at the tables,
The kine in the shed and the horse in the stables—
To pitch her sides and go over her cables.

Then you drive out where the storm-clouds swallow,
And the sound of your oar-blades, falling hollow,
Is all we have left through the months to follow.

Ah, what is Woman that you forsake her,
And the hearth-fire and the home-acre,
To go with the old grey Widow-maker?

A ST. HELENA LULLABY

('A Priest in spite of Himself'—*Rewards and Fairies*)

'How far is St. Helena from a little child at play?'
What makes you want to wander there with all the
world between?
Oh, Mother, call your son again or else he'll run away.
(*No one thinks of winter when the grass is green!*)

'How far is St. Helena from a fight in Paris Street?'
I haven't time to answer now—the men are falling fast.
The guns begin to thunder, and the drums begin to beat.
(*If you take the first step, you will take the last!*)

'How far is St. Helena from the field of Austerlitz?'
You couldn't hear me if I told—so loud the cannon roar.
But not so far for people who are living by their wits.
('*Gay go up*' means '*Gay go down*' *the wide world o'er!*)

'How far is St. Helena from an Emperor of France?'
I cannot see—I cannot tell—the Crowns they dazzle so.
The Kings sit down to dinner, and the Queens stand up to
      dance.
(*After open weather you may look for snow!*)

'How far is St. Helena from the Capes of Trafalgar?'
A longish way—a longish way—with ten year more to run.
It's South across the water underneath a falling star.
(*What you cannot finish you must leave undone!*)

'How far is St. Helena from the Beresina ice?'
An ill way—a chill way—the ice begins to crack.
But not so far for gentlemen who never took advice.
(*When you can't go forward you must e'en come back!*)

'How far is St. Helena from the field of Waterloo?'
A near way—a clear way—the ship will take you soon
A pleasant place for gentlemen with little left to do.
(*Morning never tries you till the afternoon!*)

'How far from St. Helena to the Gate of Heaven's Grace?'
That no one knows—that no one knows—and no one ever
      will.
But fold your hands across your heart and cover up your
      face,
And after all your trapesings, child, lie still!

ROAD-SONG OF THE *BANDAR-LOG*

('Kaa's Hunting'—*The Jungle Book*)

Here we go in a flung festoon,
    Half-way up to the jealous moon!
Don't you envy our pranceful bands?
Don't you wish you had extra hands?
Wouldn't you like if your tails were—*so*—
Curved in the shape of a Cupid's bow?
        Now you're angry, but—never mind,
        Brother, thy tail hangs down behind!

Here we sit in a branchy row,
Thinking of beautiful things we know;
Dreaming of deeds that we mean to do,
All complete, in a minute or two—
Something noble and grand and good,
Won by merely wishing we could.
        Now we're going to—never mind,
        Brother, thy tail hangs down behind!

All the talk we ever have heard
Uttered by bat or beast or bird—
Hide or fin or scale or feather—
Jabber it quickly and all together!
Excellent! Wonderful! Once again!
Now we are talking just like men.
        Let's pretend we are . . . Never mind!
        Brother, thy tail hangs down behind!
        This is the way of the Monkey-kind!

Then join our leaping lines that scumfish through the pines,
That rocket by where, light and high, the wild-grape swings.
By the rubbish in our wake, and the noble noise we make,
Be sure—be sure, we're going to do some splendid things!

A BRITISH-ROMAN SONG

(A.D. 406)

('A Centurion of the Thirtieth'—*Puck of Pook's Hill*)

My father's father saw it not,
    And I, belike, shall never come
To look on that so-holy spot—
        The very Rome—

Crowned by all Time, all Art, all Might,
    The equal work of Gods and Man,
City beneath whose oldest height—
        The Race began!

Soon to send forth again a brood,
    Unshakeable, we pray, that clings
To Rome's thrice-hammered hardihood—
        In arduous things.

Strong heart with triple armour bound,
    Beat strongly, for thy life-blood runs,
Age after Age, the Empire round—
        In us thy Sons

Who, distant from the Seven Hills,
    Loving and serving much, require
Thee—*thee* to guard 'gainst home-born ills
        The Imperial Fire!

A PICT SONG

('The Winged Hats'—*Puck of Pook's Hill*)

Rome never looks where she treads.
　　Always her heavy hooves fall
On our stomachs, our hearts or our heads;
　　And Rome never heeds when we bawl.
Her sentries pass on—that is all,
　　And we gather behind them in hordes,
And plot to reconquer the Wall,
　　With only our tongues for our swords.

We are the Little Folk—we!
　　Too little to love or to hate.
Leave us alone and you'll see
　　How we can drag down the State!
We are the worm in the wood!
　　We are the rot at the root!
We are the taint in the blood!
　　We are the thorn in the foot!

Mistletoe killing an oak—
　　Rats gnawing cables in two—
Moths making holes in a cloak—
　　How they must love what they do!
Yes—and we Little Folk too,
　　We are busy as they—
Working our works out of view—
　　Watch, and you'll see it some day!

No indeed! We are not strong,
　　But we know Peoples that are.
Yes, and we'll guide them along
　　To smash and destroy you in War

We shall be slaves just the same?
  Yes, we have always been slaves,
But you—you will die of the shame,
  And then we shall dance on your graves!

  We are the Little Folk, we, etc.

THE LAW OF THE JUNGLE

('How Fear Came'—*The Second Jungle Book*)

*Now this is the Law of the Jungle—as old and as true as
    the sky;
And the Wolf that shall keep it may prosper, but the Wolf
    that shall break it must die.*

*As the creeper that girdles the tree-trunk the Law runneth
    forward and back—
For the strength of the Pack is the Wolf, and the strength of
    the Wolf is the Pack.*

Wash daily from nose-tip to tail-tip; drink deeply, but
    never too deep;
And remember the night is for hunting, and forget not the
    day is for sleep.

The Jackal may follow the Tiger, but, Cub, when thy
    whiskers are grown,
Remember the Wolf is a hunter—go forth and get food of
    thine own.

Keep peace with the Lords of the Jungle—the Tiger, the
    Panther, the Bear;
And trouble not Hathi the Silent, and mock not the Boar
    in his lair.

When Pack meets with Pack in the Jungle, and neither will
go from the trail,
Lie down till the leaders have spoken—it may be fair words
shall prevail.

When ye fight with a Wolf of the Pack, ye must fight him
alone and afar,
Lest others take part in the quarrel, and the Pack be
diminished by war.

The Lair of the Wolf is his refuge, and where he has made
him his home,
Not even the Head Wolf may enter, not even the Council
may come.

The Lair of the Wolf is his refuge, but where he has digged
it too plain,
The Council shall send him a message, and so he shall
change it again.

If ye kill before midnight, be silent, and wake not the
woods with your bay,
Lest ye frighten the deer from the crops, and the brothers
go empty away.

Ye may kill for yourselves, and your mates, and your cubs
as they need, and ye can;
But kill not for pleasure of killing, and *seven times never
kill Man!*

If ye plunder his Kill from a weaker, devour not all in thy
pride;
Pack-Right is the right of the meanest; so leave him the
head and the hide.

The Kill of the Pack is the meat of the Pack. Ye must eat
where it lies;
And no one may carry away of that meat to his lair, or he
dies.

The Kill of the Wolf is the meat of the Wolf. He may do
what he will,
But, till he has given permission, the Pack may not eat of
that Kill.

Cub-Right is the right of the Yearling. From all of his
Pack he may claim
Full-gorge when the killer has eaten; and none may refuse
him the same.

Lair-Right is the right of the Mother. From all of her year
she may claim
One haunch of each kill for her litter; and none may deny
her the same.

Cave-Right is the right of the Father—to hunt by himself
for his own:
He is freed of all calls to the Pack; he is judged by the
Council alone.

Because of his age and his cunning, because of his gripe
and his paw,
In all that the Law leaveth open, the word of the Head
Wolf is Law.

*Now these are the Laws of the Jungle, and many and mighty
are they;
But the head and the hoof of the Law and the haunch and the
hump is—Obey!*

MACDONOUGH'S SONG

('As Easy as A B C'—*A Diversity of Creatures*)

Whether the State can loose and bind
  In Heaven as well as on Earth:
If it be wiser to kill mankind
  Before or after the birth—
These are matters of high concern
  Where State-kept schoolmen are;
But Holy State (we have lived to learn)
  Endeth in Holy War.

Whether The People be led by The Lord,
  Or lured by the loudest throat:
If it be quicker to die by the sword
  Or cheaper to die by vote—
These are things we have dealt with once,
  (And they will not rise from their grave)
For Holy People, however it runs,
  Endeth in wholly Slave.

Whatsoever, for any cause,
  Seeketh to take or give
Power above or beyond the Laws,
  Suffer it not to live!
Holy State or Holy King—
  Or Holy People's Will—
Have no truck with the senseless thing.
  Order the guns and kill!
    Saying—after—me:—

Once there was The People—Terror gave it birth;
Once there was The People and it made a Hell of Earth.
Earth arose and crushed it. Listen, O ye slain!
Once there was The People—it shall never be again!

THE HERITAGE

Our Fathers in a wondrous age,
   Ere yet the Earth was small,
Ensured to us an heritage,
   And doubted not at all
That we, the children of their heart,
   Which then did beat so high,
In later time should play like part
   For our posterity.

A thousand years they steadfast built,
   To 'vantage us and ours,
The Walls that were a world's despair,
   The sea-constraining Towers:
Yet in their midmost pride they knew,
   And unto Kings made known,
Not all from these their strength they drew,
   Their faith from brass or stone.

Youth's passion, manhood's fierce intent.
   With age's judgment wise,
They spent, and counted not they spent,
   At daily sacrifice.
Not lambs alone nor purchased doves
   Or tithe of trader's gold—
Their lives most dear, their dearer loves,
   They offered up of old.

Refraining e'en from lawful things,
   They bowed the neck to bear
The unadornèd yoke that brings
   Stark toil and sternest care.
Wherefore through them is Freedom sure;
   Wherefore through them we stand,
From all but sloth and pride secure,
   In a delightsome land.

Then, fretful, murmur not they gave
   So great a charge to keep,
Nor dream that awestruck Time shall save
   Their labour while we sleep.
Dear-bought and clear, a thousand year,
   Our fathers' title runs.
Make we likewise their sacrifice,
   Defrauding not our sons.

SONG OF THE FIFTH RIVER

('The Treasure and the Law'—*Puck of Pook's Hill*)

When first by Eden Tree
   The Four Great Rivers ran,
To each was appointed a Man
Her Prince and Ruler to be.

But after this was ordained
(The ancient legends tell),
There came dark Israel,
For whom no River remained.

Then He Whom the Rivers obey
Said to him: 'Fling on the ground
A handful of yellow clay,
And a Fifth Great River shall run,
Mightier than these Four,
In secret the Earth around;
And Her secret evermore
Shall be shown to thee and thy Race.'

So it was said and done.
And, deep in the veins of Earth,
And, fed by a thousand springs
That comfort the market-place,

270

Or sap the power of Kings,
The Fifth Great River had birth,
Even as it was foretold—
The Secret River of Gold!

And Israel laid down
His sceptre and his crown,
To brood on that River bank,
Where the waters flashed and sank
And burrowed in earth and fell,
And bided a season below,
For reason that none might know,
Save only Israel.

He is Lord of the Last—
The Fifth, most wonderful, Flood.
He hears Her thunder past
And Her Song is in his blood.
He can foresay: 'She will fall,'
For he knows which fountain dries
Behind which desert-belt
A thousand leagues to the South.

He can foresay: 'She will rise.'
He knows what far snows melt
Along what mountain-wall
A thousand leagues to the North.
He snuffs the coming drouth
As he snuffs the coming rain,
He knows what each will bring forth,
And turns it to his gain.

A Ruler without a Throne,
A Prince without a Sword,
Israel follows his quest.
In every land a guest,

Of many lands a lord,
In no land King is he.
But the Fifth Great River keeps
The secret of Her deeps
For Israel alone.
As it was ordered to be.

THE CHILDREN'S SONG

(*Puck of Pook's Hill*)

Land of our Birth, we pledge to thee
Our love and toil in the years to be;
When we are grown and take our place
As men and women with our race.

Father in Heaven who lovest all,
Oh, help Thy children when they call;
That they may build from age to age
An undefilèd heritage.

Teach us to bear the yoke in youth,
With steadfastness and careful truth;
That, in our time, Thy Grace may give
The Truth whereby the Nations live.

Teach us to rule ourselves alway,
Controlled and cleanly night and day;
That we may bring, if need arise,
No maimed or worthless sacrifice.

Teach us to look in all our ends
On Thee for judge, and not our friends;
That we, with Thee, may walk uncowed
By fear or favour of the crowd.

Teach us the Strength that cannot seek,
By deed or thought, to hurt the weak;
That, under Thee, we may possess
Man's strength to comfort man's distress.

Teach us Delight in simple things,
And Mirth that has no bitter springs;
Forgiveness free of evil done,
And Love to all men 'neath the sun!

Land of our Birth, our faith, our pride,
For whose dear sake our fathers died;
Oh, Motherland, we pledge to thee
Head, heart, and hand through the years to be!

IF——

('Brother Square-Toes'—*Rewards and Fairies*)

If you can keep your head when all about you
  Are losing theirs and blaming it on you,
If you can trust yourself when all men doubt you.
  But make allowance for their doubting too;
If you can wait and not be tired by waiting,
  Or being lied about, don't deal in lies,
Or being hated, don't give way to hating,
  And yet don't look too good, nor talk too wise:

If you can dream—and not make dreams your master
  If you can think—and not make thoughts your aim
If you can meet with Triumph and Disaster
  And treat those two impostors just the same;
If you can bear to hear the truth you've spoken
  Twisted by knaves to make a trap for fools.
Or watch the things you gave your life to, broken,
  And stoop and build 'em up with worn-out tools:

273

If you can make one heap of all your winnings
    And risk it on one turn of pitch-and-toss,
And lose, and start again at your beginnings
    And never breathe a word about your loss;
If you can force your heart and nerve and sinew
    To serve your turn long after they are gone,
And so hold on when there is nothing in you
    Except the Will which says to them: 'Hold on!'

If you can talk with crowds and keep your virtue,
    Or walk with Kings—nor lose the common touch,
If neither foes nor loving friends can hurt you,
    If all men count with you, but none too much;
If you can fill the unforgiving minute
    With sixty seconds' worth of distance run,
Yours is the Earth and everything that's in it,
    And—which is more—you'll be a Man, my son!

A TRANSLATION

HORACE, Bk. V, Ode 3

('Regulus'—*A Diversity of Creatures*)

There are whose study is of smells,
    And to attentive schools rehearse
How something mixed with something else
    Makes something worse.

Some cultivate in broths impure
    The clients of our body—these,
Increasing without Venus, cure,
    Or cause, disease.

274

Others the heated wheel extol,
  And all its offspring, whose concern
Is how to make it farthest roll
  And fastest turn.

Me, much incurious if the hour
  Present, or to be paid for, brings
Me to Brundusium by the power
  Of wheels or wings;

Me, in whose breast no flame hath burned
  Life-long, save that by Pindar lit,
Such lore leaves cold. I am not turned
  Aside to it

More than when, sunk in thought profound
  Of what the unaltering Gods require,
My steward (friend but slave) brings round
  Logs for my fire.

THE LAND

('Friendly Brook'—*A Diversity of Creatures*)

When Julius Fabricius, Sub-Prefect of the Weald,
  In the days of Diocletian owned our Lower River-
    field,
He called to him Hobdenius—a Briton of the Clay,
Saying: 'What about that River-piece for layin' in to
    hay?'

And the aged Hobden answered: 'I remember as a lad
My father told your father that she wanted dreenin' bad.

An' the more that you neeglect her the less you'll get her
　　clean.
Have it jest *as* you've a mind to, but, if I was you, I'd
　　dreen.'

So they drained it long and crossways in the lavish Roman
　　style—
Still we find among the river-drift their flakes of ancient
　　tile,
And in drouthy middle August, when the bones of
　　meadows show,
We can trace the lines they followed sixteen hundred years
　　ago.

Then Julius Fabricius died as even Prefects do,
And after certain centuries, Imperial Rome died too.
Then did robbers enter Britain from across the Northern
　　main
And our Lower River-field was won by Ogier the Dane.

Well could Ogier work his war-boat—well could Ogier
　　wield his brand—
Much he knew of foaming waters—not so much of farm-
　　ing land.
So he called to him a Hobden of the old unaltered blood,
Saying: 'What about that River-piece; she doesn't look
　　no good?'

And that aged Hobden answered: ''Tain't for *me* to
　　interfere,
But I've known that bit o' meadow now for five and fifty
　　year.
Have it *jest* as you've a mind to, but I've proved it time on
　　time,
If you want to change her nature you have *got* to give
　　her lime!'

Ogier sent his wains to Lewes, twenty hours' solemn walk,
And drew back great abundance of the cool, grey, healing
    chalk,
And old Hobden spread it broadcast, never heeding what
    was in't.—
Which is why in cleaning ditches, now and then we find a
    flint.

Ogier died. His sons grew English—Anglo-Saxon was
    their name—
Till out of blossomed Normandy another pirate came;
For Duke William conquered England and divided with
    his men,
And our Lower River-field he gave to William of Warenne.

But the Brook (you know her habit) rose one rainy autumn
    night
And tore down sodden flitches of the bank to left and
    right.
So, said William to his Bailiff as they rode their dripping
    rounds:
'Hob, what about that River-bit—the Brook's got up no
    bounds?'

And that aged Hobden answered: ''Tain't my business to
    advise,
But ye might ha' known 'twould happen from the way the
    valley lies.
Where ye can't hold back the water you must try and save
    the sile.
Hev it jest as you've a *mind* to, but, if I was you, I'd spile!'

They spiled along the water-course with trunks of willow-
    trees,
And planks of elms behind 'em and immortal oaken knees.

And when the spates of Autumn whirl the gravel-beds
    away
You can see their faithful fragments, iron-hard in iron clay.

.   .   .   .

Georgii Quinti Anno Sexto, I, who own the River-field,
Am fortified with title-deeds, attested, signed and sealed,
Guaranteeing me, my assigns, my executors and heirs
All sorts of powers and profits which—are neither mine
    nor theirs.

I have rights of chase and warren, as my dignity requires.
I can fish—but Hobden tickles. I can shoot—but Hobden
    wires.
I repair, but he reopens, certain gaps which, men allege,
Have been used by every Hobden since a Hobden swapped
    a hedge.

Shall I dog his morning progress o'er the track-betraying
    dew?
Demand his dinner-basket into which my pheasant flew?
Confiscate his evening faggot under which my conies ran,
And summons him to judgment? I would sooner sum-
    mons Pan.

His dead are in the churchyard—thirty generations laid.
Their names were old in history when Domesday Book
    was made;
And the passion and the piety and prowess of his line
Have seeded, rooted, fruited in some land the Law calls
    mine.

Not for any beast that burrows, not for any bird that flies.
Would I lose his large sound counsel, miss his keen amend-
    ing eyes.
He is bailiff, woodman, wheelwright, field-surveyor,
    engineer,
And if flagrantly a poacher—'tain't for me to interfere.

'Hob, what about that River-bit?' I turn to him again,
With Fabricius and Ogier and William of Warenne.
'Hev it jest as you've a mind to, *but*'—and here he takes
    command.
For whoever pays the taxes old Mus' Hobden owns the
    land.

THE QUEEN'S MEN

('Gloriana'—*Rewards and Fairies*)

Valour and Innocence
  Have latterly gone hence
To certain death by certain shame attended.
Envy—ah! even to tears!—
The fortune of their years
Which, though so few, yet so divinely ended.

Scarce had they lifted up
Life's full and fiery cup,
Than they had set it down untouched before them.
Before their day arose
They beckoned it to close—
Close in confusion and destruction o'er them.

They did not stay to ask
What prize should crown their task—
Well sure that prize was such as no man strives for;
But passed into eclipse,
Her kiss upon their lips—
Even Belphœbe's, whom they gave their lives for!

MINE SWEEPERS

1914-18

(*Sea Warfare*)

Dawn off the Foreland—the young flood making
  Jumbled and short and steep—
Black in the hollows and bright where it's breaking—
  Awkward water to sweep.
    'Mines reported in the fairway,
    'Warn all traffic and detain.
  ''Sent up *Unity*, *Claribel*, *Assyrian*, *Stormcock*, and *Golden Gain.*'

Noon off the Foreland—the first ebb making
  Lumpy and strong in the bight.
Boom after boom, and the golf-hut shaking
  And the jackdaws wild with fright!
    'Mines located in the fairway,
    'Boats now working up the chain,
  'Sweepers—*Unity*, *Claribel*, *Assyrian*, *Stormcock*, and
    Golden Gain.'

Dusk off the Foreland—the last light going
  And the traffic crowding through,
And five damned trawlers with their syreens blowing
  Heading the whole review!
    'Sweep completed in the fairway.
    'No more mines remain.
  ''Sent back *Unity*, *Claribel*, *Assyrian*, *Stormcock*, and
    Golden Gain.'

THE LOVE SONG OF HAR DYAL

('Beyond the Pale'—*Plain Tales from the Hills*)

Alone upon the housetops to the North
  I turn and watch the lightnings in the sky—
The glamour of thy footsteps in the North.
Come back to me, Beloved, or I die!

Below my feet the still bazar is laid—
Far, far below the weary camels lie—
The camels and the captives of thy raid.
Come back to me, Beloved, or I die!

My father's wife is old and harsh with years,
And drudge of all my father's house am I—
My bread is sorrow and my drink is tears.
Come back to me, Beloved, or I die!

MOWGLI'S SONG AGAINST PEOPLE

('Letting in the Jungle'—*The Second Jungle Book*)

I will let loose against you the fleet-footed vines—
I will call in the Jungle to stamp out your lines!
  The roofs shall fade before it,
    The house-beams shall fall;
  And the *Karela*,[1] the bitter *Karela*,
    Shall cover it all!

In the gates of these your councils my people shall sing.
In the doors of these your garners the Bat-folk shall cling;
  And the snake shall be your watchman,
    By a hearthstone unswept;
  For the *Karela*, the bitter *Karela*,
    Shall fruit where ye slept!

[1] A wild melon.

281

Ye shall not see my strikers; ye shall hear them and guess.
By night, before the moon-rise, I will send for my cess,
And the wolf shall be your herdsman
By a landmark removed;
For the *Karela*, the bitter *Karela*,
Shall seed where ye loved!

I will reap your fields before you at the hands of a host.
Ye shall glean behind my reapers for the bread that is
lost;
And the deer shall be your oxen
On a headland untilled;
For the *Karela*, the bitter *Karela*,
Shall leaf where ye build!

I have untied against you the club-footed vines—
I have sent in the Jungle to swamp out your lines!
The trees—the trees are on you!
The house-beams shall fall;
And the *Karela*, the bitter *Karela*,
Shall cover you all!

'THE TRADE'

1914–18

(*Sea Warfare*)

They bear, in place of classic names,
Letters and numbers on their skin.
They play their grisly blindfold games
In little boxes made of tin.
Sometimes they stalk the Zeppelin,
Sometimes they learn where mines are laid,
Or where the Baltic ice is thin.
That is the custom of 'The Trade'.

Few prize-courts sit upon their claims.
  They seldom tow their targets in.
They follow certain secret aims
  Down under, far from strife or din.
  When they are ready to begin
No flag is flown, no fuss is made
  More than the shearing of a pin.
That is the custom of 'The Trade'.

The Scout's quadruple funnel flames
  A mark from Sweden to the Swin,
The Cruiser's thund'rous screw proclaims
  Her comings out and goings in:
  But only whiffs of paraffin
Or creamy rings that fizz and fade
  Show where the one-eyed Death has been.
That is the custom of 'The Trade'.

Their feats, their fortunes and their fames
  Are hidden from their nearest kin;
No eager public backs or blames,
  No journal prints the yarn they spin
  (The Censor would not let it in!)
When they return from run or raid.
  Unheard they work, unseen they win.
That is the custom of 'The Trade'.

THE RUNES ON WELAND'S SWORD
1906

('Old Men at Pevensey'—*Puck of Pook's Hill*)

A Smith makes me
  To betray my Man
In my first fight.

283

To gather Gold
At the world's end
I am sent.

The Gold I gather
Comes into England
Out of deep Water.

Like a shining Fish
Then it descends
Into deep Water.

It is not given
For goods or gear,
But for The Thing.

The Gold I gather
A king covets
For an ill use.

The Gold I gather
Is drawn up
Out of deep Water.

Like a shining Fish
Then it descends
Into deep Water.

It is not given
For goods or gear,
But for The Thing.

SONG OF THE GALLEY-SLAVES

(' "The Finest Story in the World" '—*Many Inventions*)

We pulled for you when the wind was against us and the sails were low.
> *Will you never let us go?*

We ate bread and onions when you took towns, or ran aboard quickly when you were beaten back by the foe.

The Captains walked up and down the deck in fair weather singing songs, but we were below.

We fainted with our chins on the oars and you did not see that we were idle, for we still swung to and fro.
> *Will you never let us go?*

The salt made the oar-handles like shark-skin; our knees were cut to the bone with salt-cracks; our hair was stuck to our foreheads; and our lips were cut to the gums, and you whipped us because we could not row.
> *Will you never let us go?*

But, in a little time, we shall run out of the port-holes as the water runs along the oar-blade, and though you tell the others to row after us you will never catch us till you catch the oar-thresh and tie up the winds in the belly of the sail. Aho!
> *Will you never let us go?*

THE ROMAN CENTURION'S SONG

(ROMAN OCCUPATION OF BRITAIN, A.D. 300)

Legate, I had the news last night—my cohort ordered home
By ship to Portus Itius and thence by road to Rome

285

I've marched the companies aboard, the arms are stowed
    below:
Now let another take my sword. Command me not to go!

I've served in Britain forty years, from Vectis to the
    Wall.
I have none other home than this, nor any life at all.
Last night I did not understand, but, now the hour draws
    near
That calls me to my native land, I feel that land is here.

Here where men say my name was made, here where my
    work was done;
Here where my dearest dead are laid—my wife—my wife
    and son;
Here where time, custom, grief and toil, age, memory,
    service, love,
Have rooted me in British soil. Ah, how can I remove?

For me this land, that sea, these airs, those folk and fields
    suffice.
What purple Southern pomp can match our changeful
    Northern skies,
Black with December snows unshed or pearled with
    August haze—
The clanging arch of steel-grey March, or June's long-
    lighted days?

You'll follow widening Rhodanus till vine and olive
    lean
Aslant before the sunny breeze that sweeps Nemausus
    clean
To Arelate's triple gate; but let me linger on,
Here where our stiff-necked British oaks confront Euro-
    clydon!

You'll take the old Aurelian Road through shore-descending pines
Where, blue as any peacock's neck, the Tyrrhene Ocean shines.
You'll go where laurel crowns are won, but—will you e'er forget.
The scent of hawthorn in the sun, or bracken in the wet?

Let me work here for Britain's sake—at any task you will—
A marsh to drain, a road to make or native troops to drill.
Some Western camp (I know the Pict) or granite Border keep,
Mid seas of heather derelict, where our old messmates sleep..

Legate, I come to you in tears—My cohort ordered home!
I've served in Britain forty years. What should I do in Rome?
Here is my heart, my soul, my mind—the only life I know.
I cannot leave it all behind. Command me not to go!

DANE-GELD

(A.D. 980–1016)

It is always a temptation to an armed and agile nation
  To call upon a neighbour and to say:—
'We invaded you last night—we are quite prepared to fight,
  Unless you pay us cash to go away.'

  And that is called asking for Dane-geld,
    And the people who ask it explain
  That you've only to pay 'em the Dane-geld
    And then you'll get rid of the Dane!

287

It is always a temptation to a rich and lazy nation,
   To puff and look important and to say:—
'Though we know we should defeat you, we have not the
      time to meet you.
We will therefore pay you cash to go away.'

And that is called paying the Dane-geld;
   But we've proved it again and again,
That if once you have paid him the Dane-geld
   You never get rid of the Dane.

It is wrong to put temptation in the path of any nation,
   For fear they should succumb and go astray;
So when you are requested to pay up or be molested,
   You will find it better policy to say:—

'We never pay *any*-one Dane-geld,
   No matter how trifling the cost;
For the end of that game is oppression and shame,
   And the nation that plays it is lost!'

NORMAN AND SAXON

(A.D. 1100)

'My son,' said the Norman Baron, 'I am dying, and
   you will be heir
To all the broad acres in England that William gave me
   for my share
When we conquered the Saxon at Hastings, and a nice
   little handful it is.
But before you go over to rule it I want you to understand
   this:—

'The Saxon is not like us Normans. His manners are not
      so polite.
But he never means anything serious till he talks about
      justice and right.
When he stands like an ox in the furrow with his sullen
      set eyes on your own,
And grumbles, "This isn't fair dealing," my son, leave the
      Saxon alone.

'You can horsewhip your Gascony archers, or torture
      your Picardy spears;
But don't try that game on the Saxon; you'll have the
      whole brood round your ears.
From the richest old Thane in the county to the poorest
      chained serf in the field,
They'll be at you and on you like hornets, and, if you are
      wise, you will yield.

'But first you must master their language, their dialect,
      proverbs and songs.
Don't trust any clerk to interpret when they come with the
      tale of their wrongs.
Let them know that you know what they're saying; let
      them feel that you know what to say.
Yes, even when you want to go hunting, hear 'em out if it
      takes you all day.

'They'll drink every hour of the daylight and poach every
      hour of the dark.
It's the sport not the rabbits they're after (we've plenty of
      game in the park).
Don't hang them or cut off their fingers. That's wasteful
      as well as unkind,
For a hard-bitten, South-country poacher makes the best
      man-at-arms you can find.

' Appear with your wife and the children at their weddings
    and funerals and feasts.
Be polite but not friendly to Bishops; be good to all poor
    parish priests.
Say "we," "us" and "ours" when you're talking, instead
    of "you fellows" and "I."
Don't ride over seeds; keep your temper; and *never you
    tell 'em a lie!*'

EDGEHILL FIGHT

(CIVIL WARS, 1642)

Naked and grey the Cotswolds stand
    Beneath the autumn sun,
And the stubble-fields on either hand
    Where Stour and Avon run.
There is no change in the patient land
    That has bred us every one.

She should have passed in cloud and fire
    And saved us from this sin
Of war—red war—'twixt child and sire,
    Household and kith and kin,
In the heart of a sleepy Midland shire,
    With the harvest scarcely in.

But there is no change as we meet at last
    On the brow-head or the plain,
And the raw astonished ranks stand fast
    To slay or to be slain
By the men they knew in the kindly past
    That shall never come again—

By the men they met at dance or chase,
    In the tavern or the hall,
At the justice-bench and the market-place,
    At the cudgel-play or brawl—
Of their own blood and speech and race,
    Comrades or neighbours all!

More bitter than death this day must prove
    Whichever way it go,
For the brothers of the maids we love
    Make ready to lay low
Their sisters' sweethearts, as we move
    Against our dearest foe.

Thank Heaven! At last the trumpets peal
    Before our strength gives way.
For King or for the Commonweal—
    No matter which they say,
The first dry rattle of new-drawn steel
    Changes the world to-day!

THE DUTCH IN THE MEDWAY

(1664–72)

If wars were won by feasting,
    Or victory by song,
Or safety found in sleeping sound,
    How England would be strong!
But honour and dominion
    Are not maintained so.
They're only got by sword and shot,
    And this the Dutchmen know!

The moneys that should feed us
  You spend on your delight,
How can you then have sailor-men
  To aid you in your fight?
Our fish and cheese are rotten,
  Which makes the scurvy grow—
We cannot serve you if we starve,
  And this the Dutchmen know!

Our ships in every harbour
  Be neither whole nor sound,
And when we seek to mend a leak,
  No oakum can be found;
Or, if it is, the caulkers,
  And carpenters also,
For lack of pay have gone away,
  And this the Dutchmen know!

Mere powder, guns, and bullets,
  We scarce can get at all;
Their price was spent in merriment
  And revel at Whitehall,
While we in tattered doublets
  From ship to ship must row,
Beseeching friends for odds and ends—
  And this the Dutchmen know!

No King will heed our warnings,
  No Court will pay our claims—
Our King and Court for their disport
  Do sell the very Thames!
For, now De Ruyter's topsails
  Off naked Chatham show,
We dare not meet him with our fleet—
  And this the Dutchmen know!

THE SECRET OF THE MACHINES

(MODERN MACHINERY)

We were taken from the ore-bed and the mine,
   We were melted in the furnace and the pit—
We were cast and wrought and hammered to design,
   We were cut and filed and tooled and gauged to fit.
Some water, coal, and oil is all we ask,
   And a thousandth of an inch to give us play:
And now, if you will set us to our task,
   We will serve you four and twenty hours a day!

     We can pull and haul and push and lift and drive,
     We can print and plough and weave and heat and
       light,
     We can run and race and swim and fly and dive,
     We can see and hear and count and read and write!

Would you call a friend from half across the world?
   If you'll let us have his name and town and state,
You shall see and hear your crackling question hurled
   Across the arch of heaven while you wait.
Has he answered? Does he need you at his side?
   You can start this very evening if you choose,
And take the Western Ocean in the stride
   Of seventy thousand horses and some screws!

     The boat-express is waiting your command!
     You will find the *Mauretania* at the quay,
     Till her captain turns the lever 'neath his hand,
     And the monstrous nine-decked city goes to sea.

Do you wish to make the mountains bare their head
   And lay their new-cut forests at your feet?
Do you want to turn a river in its bed,
   Or plant a barren wilderness with wheat?

Shall we pipe aloft and bring you water down
　From the never-failing cisterns of the snows,
To work the mills and tramways in your town,
　And irrigate your orchards as it flows?

　　It is easy! Give us dynamite and drills!
　　Watch the iron-shouldered rocks lie down and quake,
　　As the thirsty desert-level floods and fills,
　　And the valley we have dammed becomes a lake.

But remember, please, the Law by which we live,
　We are not built to comprehend a lie,
We can neither love nor pity nor forgive.
　If you make a slip in handling us you die!
We are greater than the Peoples or the Kings—
　Be humble, as you crawl beneath our rods!—
Our touch can alter all created things,
　We are everything on earth—except The Gods!

　　Though our smoke may hide the Heavens from your
　　　eyes,
　　It will vanish and the stars will shine again,
　　Because, for all our power and weight and size,
　　We are nothing more than children of your brain!

GERTRUDE'S PRAYER

('Dayspring Mishandled')

That which is marred at birth Time shall not mend,
　Nor water out of bitter well make clean;
All evil thing returneth at the end,
　Or elseway walketh in our blood unseen.
Whereby the more is sorrow in certaine—
Dayspring mishandled cometh not againe.

To-bruizèd be that slender, sterting spray
    Out of the oake's rind that should betide
A branch of girt and goodliness, straightway
    Her spring is turnèd on herself, and wried
And knotted like some gall or veiney wen.—
Dayspring mishandled cometh not agen.

Noontide repayeth never morning-bliss—
    Sith noon to morn is incomparable;
And, so it be our dawning goth amiss,
    None other after-hour serveth well.
Ah! Jesu-Moder, pitie my oe paine—
Dayspring mishandled cometh not againe!

THE GODS OF THE COPYBOOK HEADINGS

1919

As I pass through my incarnations in every age and
    race,
I make my proper prostrations to the Gods of the Market-
    Place.
Peering through reverent fingers I watch them flourish and
    fall,
And the Gods of the Copybook Headings, I notice, outlast
    them all.

We were living in trees when they met us. They showed us
    each in turn
That Water would certainly wet us, as Fire would certainly
    burn:
But we found them lacking in Uplift, Vision and Breadth
    of Mind,
So we left them to teach the Gorillas while we followed
    the March of Mankind.

We moved as the Spirit listed. *They* never altered their
pace,
Being neither cloud nor wind-borne like the Gods of the
Market-Place;
But they always caught up with our progress, and presently
word would come
That a tribe had been wiped off its icefield, or the lights
had gone out in Rome.

With the Hopes that our World is built on they were
utterly out of touch,
They denied that the Moon was Stilton; they denied she
was even Dutch.
They denied that Wishes were Horses; they denied that a
Pig had Wings.
So we worshipped the Gods of the Market Who promised
these beautiful things.

When the Cambrian measures were forming, They prom-
ised perpetual peace.
They swore, if we gave them our weapons, that the wars of
the tribes would cease.
But when we disarmed They sold us and delivered us
bound to our foe,
And the Gods of the Copybook Headings said: '*Stick to
the Devil you know.*'

On the first Feminian Sandstones we were promised the
Fuller Life
(Which started by loving our neighbour and ended by
loving his wife)
Till our women had no more children and the men lost
reason and faith,
And the Gods of the Copybook Headings said: '*The
Wages of Sin is Death.*'

296

In the Carboniferous Epoch we were promised abundance
for all,
By robbing selected Peter to pay for collective Paul;
But, though we had plenty of money, there was nothing
our money could buy,
And the Gods of the Copybook Headings said: '*If you
don't work you die.*'

Then the Gods of the Market tumbled, and their smooth-
tongued wizards withdrew,
And the hearts of the meanest were humbled and began to
believe it was true
That All is not Gold that Glitters, and Two and Two
make Four—
And the Gods of the Copybook Headings limped up to
explain it once more.

.   .   .   .   .

As it will be in the future, it was at the birth of Man—
There are only four things certain since Social Progress
began:—
That the Dog returns to his Vomit and the Sow returns to
her Mire,
And the burnt Fool's bandaged finger goes wabbling back
to the Fire;

And that after this is accomplished, and the brave new
world begins
When all men are paid for existing and no man must pay
for his sins,
As surely as Water will wet us, as surely as Fire will burn,
The Gods of the Copybook Headings with terror and
slaughter return!

THE STORM CONE
1932

This is the midnight—let no star
Delude us—dawn is very far.
This is the tempest long foretold—
Slow to make head but sure to hold.

Stand by! The lull 'twixt blast and blast
Signals the storm is near, not past;
And worse than present jeopardy
May our forlorn to-morrow be.

If we have cleared the expectant reef,
Let no man look for his relief.
Only the darkness hides the shape
Of further peril to escape.

It is decreed that we abide
The weight of gale against the tide
And those huge waves the outer main
Sends in to set us back again.

They fall and whelm. We strain to hear
The pulses of her labouring gear,
Till the deep throb beneath us proves,
After each shudder and check, she moves!

She moves, with all save purpose lost,
To make her offing from the coast;
But, till she fetches open sea,
Let no man deem that he is free!

THE APPEAL

IF I HAVE GIVEN YOU DELIGHT
 BY AUGHT THAT I HAVE DONE,
LET ME LIE QUIET IN THAT NIGHT
 WHICH SHALL BE YOURS ANON:

AND FOR THE LITTLE, LITTLE, SPAN
 THE DEAD ARE BORNE IN MIND,
SEEK NOT TO QUESTION OTHER THAN
 THE BOOKS I LEAVE BEHIND.

INDEX TO FIRST LINES

PAGE

A fool there was and he made his prayer . . 108
A Nation spoke to a Nation 100
A Smith makes me 283
A stone's throw out on either hand . . 252
A tinker out of Bedford 120
Ah! What avails the classic bent . . . 142
Ah, would swift ships had never been, for then we
    ne'er had found 167
Alone upon the housetops to the North . . 281
'And some are sulky, while some will plunge . . 250
As I pass through my incarnations in every age and
    race 295
As I was spittin' into the Ditch aboard o' the *Crocodile* 202
'Ave you 'eard o' the Widow at Windsor . . 181
Be well assured that on our side . . . 78
Beyond the path of the outmost sun through utter
    darkness hurled— 44
Body and Spirit I surrendered whole . . 162
Broke to every known mischance, lifted over all 122
By the old Moulmein Pagoda, lookin' lazy at the sea 187
Call me not false, beloved 167
Cities and Thrones and Powers . . . 239
Cry 'Murder' in the market-place, and each . . 249
Daily, though no ears attended . . . 165
Dawn off the Foreland—the young flood making . 280
Death favoured me from the first, well knowing I could
    not endure 163
'E was warned agin 'er— 214
Fair is our lot—O goodly is our heritage! . . 87
Faithless the watch that I kept: now I have none to
    keep 164

301

For all we have and are 140
For Fog and Fate no charm is found . . . 166
For things we never mention 48
From every quarter of your land 86
From little towns in a far land we came . . . 163
From the date that the doors of his prep-school close 258
Go, stalk the red deer o'er the heather . . . 250
God gave all men all earth to love 105
God of our fathers, known of old 139
Gods of the Nile, should this stout fellow here . . 162
'Gold is for the mistress—silver for the maid— . . 255
He drank strong waters and his speech was coarse . 252
He from the wind-bitten North with ship and com-
    panions descended 166
Headless, lacking foot and hand 166
Hear now the Song of the Dead- in the North by the
    torn berg-edges— 89
Here we go in a flung festoon 262
Here, where my fresh-turned furrows run . . 103
'How far is St. Helena from a little child at play?' . 260
I am the land of their fathers 240
I could not dig: I dared not rob 165
I could not look on Death, which being known . 162
I do not love my Empire's foes 232
I followed my Duke ere I was a lover . . . 245
I have slain none except my Mother. She . . 161
I have watched a thousand days 167
I'm 'ere in a ticky ulster an' a broken billycock 'at . 197
I'm just in love with all these three . . . 243
I've paid for your sickest fancies; I've humoured
    your crackedest whim— 66
I've taken my fun where I've found it . . . 211
'I was a Have' 161
I was a shepherd to fools 166
I was of delicate mind. I stepped aside for my needs 164
I went into a public-'ouse to get a pint o' beer . 172
I will let loose against you the fleet-footed vines— . 281
If any mourn us in the workshop, say . . . 164

302

If any question why we died 164
If I had clamoured at Thy Gate 165
If I have given you delight 299
If wars were won by feasting 291
If you can keep your head when all about you . 273
In extended observation of the ways and works of
    man 118
In the daytime, when she moved about me . . 251
It got beyond all orders an' it got beyond all 'ope . 207
It is always a temptation to an armed and agile nation 287
It was not in the open fight 251
Land of our Birth, we pledge to thee . . . 272
Laughing through clouds, his milk-teeth still unshed 164
Legate, I had the news last night—my cohort ordered
    home 285
Like as the Oak whose roots descend . . . 145
Little Blind Fish, thou art marvellous wise . . 254
Look, you have cast out Love! What Gods are these 249
Lord, Thou hast made this world below the shadow
    of a dream 57
March! The mud is cakin' good about our trousies 200
Me that 'ave been what I've been— . . . 224
My father's father saw it not 263
My girl, she give me the go onest 195
My name is O'Kelly, I've heard the Revelly . . 196
My name, my speech, my self I had forgot . . 162
My new-cut ashlar takes the light . . . 256
'My son,' said the Norman Baron, 'I am dying, and
    you will be heir' 288
My son was killed while laughing at some jest. I
    would I knew 161
Naked and grey the Cotswolds stand . . . 290
*No doubt but ye are the People—your throne is above
    the King's* 128
Non nobis Domine!— 257
Not though you die to-night, O Sweet, and wail . 250
*Now this is the Law of the Jungle—as old and as true
    as the sky* 265

303

Now Tomlinson gave up the ghost at his house in
Berkeley Square   146
Of all the trees that grow so fair   246
*Oh, East is East, and West is West, and never the twain
shall meet*   111
On the first hour of my first day   163
Once, after long-drawn revel at The Mermaid .   143
One from the ends of the earth—gifts at an open
door—   93
One used and butchered me: another spied .   .   166
Our brows are bound with spindrift and the weed is
on our knees   88
Our Fathers in a wondrous age   269
Peace is declared, an' I return   237
Pit where the buffalo cooled his hide .   .   .   252
Pity not! The Army gave   162
Pleasant it is for the Little Tin Gods .   .   .   254
Prometheus brought down fire to men .   .   .   164
Ride with an idle whip, ride with an unused heel .   251
Rome never looks where she treads .   .   .   264
Rosicrucian subtleties   253
Royal and Dower-royal, I the Queen .   .   .   94
See you the ferny ride that steals .   .   .   241
Seven men from all the world back to Docks again .   76
Smokin' my pipe on the mountings, sniffin' the
mornin'-cool   176
So we loosed a bloomin' volley   253
Speakin' in general, I 'ave tried 'em all— .   .   45
'Stopped in the straight when the race was his own!—   250
Take of English earth as much   248
Take up the White Man's burden— .   .   .   136
That which is marred at birth Time shall not mend .   294
The bachelor 'e fights for one   228
The blown sand heaps on me, that none may learn .   163
The earth is full of anger   138
The 'eathen in 'is blindness bows down to wood an'
stone   216
The Garden called Gethsemane   50

	PAGE
The General 'eard the firin' on the flank . . .	230
The Injian Ocean sets an' smiles	220
The King has called for priest and cup . . .	153
The men that fought at Minden, they was rookies in their time—	209
The overfaithful sword returns the user . . .	55
The smoke upon your Altar dies	43
The Sons of Mary seldom bother, for they have inherited that good part	159
The Weald is good, the Downs are best— . .	244
The white moth to the closing bine . . .	98
The World hath set its heavy yoke	250
The wrecks dissolve above us; their dust drops down from afar—	92
Then a pile of heads he laid	253
There are whose study is of smells . . .	274
There is a tide in the affairs of men . . .	254
There is a word you often see, pronounce it as you may—	235
There's a little red-faced man	168
There's a whisper down the field where the year has shot her yield	82
There was a row in Silver Street that's near to Dublin Quay	183
There was no one like 'im, 'Orse or Foot . .	213
They bear, in place of classic names . . .	282
They burnt a corpse upon the sand— . . .	251
They christened my brother of old— . . .	124
They shall not return to us, the resolute, the young .	127
They shut the road through the woods . . .	242
This is the midnight—let no star	298
This man in his own country prayed we know not to what Powers	162
Thus, for a season, they fought it fair . . .	253
Thus said the Lord in the Vault above the Cherubim	80
To the legion of the lost ones, to the cohort of the damned	193
To-day, across our fathers' graves	132

To-night, God knows what thing shall tide . . 252
Troopin', troopin', troopin' to the sea . . . 190
Truly ye come of The Blood; slower to bless than to ban 97
Valour and Innocence 279
We counterfeited once for your disport . . . 168
We giving all gained all 163
We have fed our sea for a thousand years . . 91
We have no heart for the fishing—we have no hand
    for the oar— 133
We knew thee of old 47
We pulled for you when the wind was against us and
    the sails were low 285
We're foot—slog—slog—slog—sloggin' over Africa! 227
We're not so old in the Army List . . . 102
We've fought with many men acrost the seas . 174
We were dreamers, dreaming greatly, in the man-
    stifled town 90
We were taken from the ore-bed and the mine . 293
We were together since the War began . . . 161
'What are the bugles blowin' for?' said Files-on-Parade 170
What is a woman that you forsake her . . . 259
When Drake went down to the Horn . . . 91
When Earth's last picture is painted and the tubes are
    twisted and dried 110
When first by Eden Tree 270
When Julius Fabricius, Sub-Prefect of the Weald . 275
When 'Omer smote 'is bloomin' lyre . . . 146
When the 'arf-made recruity goes out to the East . 185
When the earth was sick and the skies were grey . 249
When the Waters were dried an' the Earth did appear 205
When you've shouted 'Rule Britannia,' when you've
    sung 'God save the Queen' 222
Whence comest thou, Gehazi 116
'Where have you been this while away' . . . 191
Whether the State can loose and bind . . . 268
While the snaffle holds or the long-neck stings . 254
You couldn't pack a Broadwood half a mile— . 51
You may talk o' gin and beer 179